DEAF EDUCATION IN EUROPE

THE EARLY YEARS

Henk Betten

ISBN 978-90-806571-5-1

Author: Henk Betten
Publisher: Maya de Wit – Sign Language Interpreting Consultancy
Front cover: Vivian van Schagen
Back cover photograph: Fotoburo Ferdinand van der Duin

"We will explore in a sensible way how to proceed to get through the window what we cannot get through the door, that is, to seep into the deaf mutes' minds, through the eyes, what we cannot put through the ears."[1]

C.M. de l'Epée – Paris, 1784

---

[1] "On verra d'une manière sensible comment on doit s'y prendre pour faire monter par la fenêtre ce qui ne peut entrer par la porte, c'est-à-dire, pour insinuer dans l'esprit des Sourds et Muets, par le canal de leurs yeux, ce qu'on ne peut y introduire par l'ouverture de leurs oreilles."
Translated by Alexandre Le Roy, London, July 2013

I give my heartfelt thanks to everyone who provided me information, and I would especially like to thank Maya de Wit for her support to realize the book and our pleasant cooperation, also Royal Dutch Kentalis for making the translation into English possible and to use their extensive library sources. Finally, I would like to thank Hetty, my wife, Marleen, and Erik for all the support they gave me.

Henk Betten

TABLE OF CONTENTS

LIST OF FIGURES

FOREWORD

The history of Deaf people is intertwined with the history of their education. Until 1760, Deaf people in Europe only were educated incidentally: when their parents could afford a private tutor for their Deaf child or when scientists searched out Deaf persons to investigate the possibility to teach language to those who could not hear. The first initiatives to set up formal education for Deaf people occurred in Europe in 1760, resulting in the founding of schools for the Deaf in numerous European countries. However, a detailed overview of the founding of European schools for the Deaf and their communication methods has so far not been published.

This publication by Henk Betten fills the gap in knowledge on the founding of formal education of Deaf people in Europe, giving us interesting details. I heartily recommend this publication to anyone interested in the history of the education of the Deaf worldwide! Not only because this publication is very informative, but also because of the qualities of the author.

Henk Betten has dedicated himself to investigate aspects of the history of Deaf people, such as art, sports, and education, resulting in numerous publications in Dutch language and presentations at national and international congresses. Seemingly tireless, he has spent an unthinkable amount of time and effort on this task, all on his own initiative. The quality of the research of Henk Betten is always outstanding, due to his accurate and conscious approach. As a consequence, the results of his work are valuable for everybody who is interested in the history of Deaf people, from laymen to academic researchers.

Corrie Tijsseling

MSc Philosophy and History of Education
Utrecht University
The Netherlands

INTRODUCTION

From 1942 to 1955 I was an apprentice at the Institute for deaf children H.D. Guyot in Groningen, founded in 1790. As a hobby, I conducted historical research on deaf education for years. The favorite place for this research is the large library of the world famous Charles Guyot library in Haren, the Netherlands. Currently I am the librarian of this very library at Royal Dutch Kentalis (former H.D. Guyot school) in the Netherlands.

Institutes for the deaf can be found all over the world. Generally their aim is to offer education for children who are deaf or have a severe hearing disability. Formal classroom education for deaf pupils started with an initiative of Abbé Charles Michel de l'Epée. He started in 1760 in Paris to educate and establish a school for deaf people. He was the first to do so and in doing so, he brought light to the world of deaf people. Before he started teaching, deaf people were often excluded from society. Before 1760, and in some cases for many years afterwards, a deaf person was seen as a useless creature or even as an animal. Apart from the lucky ones who received individual education, many deaf people could only perform simple activities due to their lack of education.

In his teaching, De l'Epée used manual gestures and a simple finger alphabet. His method became known as manualism. His counterpart was Samuel Heinicke, who at approximately the same time was working in Germany on a different method; the pure oral method. The oral method involved learning to speak and mimicking mouth movements, while manual gestures were not allowed. De l'Epée and Heinicke kept up a correspondence in which each heavily criticized the method of the other. Nowadays, the bilingual method is used in most of the deaf schools in Europe, which combines teaching both sign language and spoken and written language to deaf children. A detailed discussion can be found in my article entitled: 'Manual method versus oral method' (Appendix 3).

De l'Epée's influence was enormous; his method led to a boom in the development of international deaf education. De l'Epée gave public demonstration lessons and he also taught hearing persons, who would subsequently establish schools for the deaf in their own countries in Europe. This was how De l'Epée's method spread. Heinicke's method did not become popular until 1850.

The effort by De L'Epée and others to release deaf people from the shackles of loneliness and poverty inspired me to make an overview of the history of schools for the deaf in Europe. I contacted deaf institutes and schools around Europe and asked them to provide me information on their history and establishment (appendix 1). Since 1988 I have been collecting this information and compiling it in this publication to provide an overview of the earliest developments of deaf education in Europe. The information in this publication is based on personal correspondence and complemented with scientific and informal publications.

Henk Betten

ALBANIA

For centuries Albania did not have any facilities for deaf, blind and disabled people. It was not until 1963 that, due to the efforts of the communist government in Russia, a school was opened in Tirana for deaf, blind, and visually disabled pupils. Later, in 1993, these pupils received instruction on an individual basis. In 1963, the school taught deaf and blind children (about 100 pupils) to communicate by means of the hand alphabet.

Figure 1: Students at the school for the Deaf in Tirana (1994)

In 1963 the Albanian government sent several teachers to Russia to gain experience teaching deaf children. Currently the state is the sole financer of this school and pays for food, clothing, and teaching materials. The teachers at this school for the deaf are paid 15 percent more than teachers at mainstream schools.

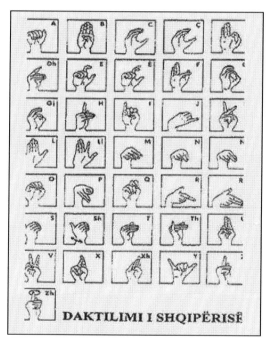

Figure 2: Albanian Hand Alphabet

Since 1996, Effatha[2] Zoetermeer in the Netherlands has supported the school for the deaf in Tirana. Ineke Hania, teacher in Zoetermeer, is the contact person for Effatha. From 1994 to 1996, she worked at the Albanian school and was actively involved with the institute.

According to the information provided by Hania, Albania has only one institute for deaf and hard of hearing children; there is a boarding school where the children also spend the weekends. In December, the students go home for two weeks and in the summer they have three and a half months holiday. In 1995, the school had 260 pupils; classes had an average of ten pupils. Parents paid €2 a month. However, due to poverty many parents could not afford to pay this. In 1998, the institute for the deaf had 200 pupils and 92 members of staff.

Sources:

Content:
Ineke Hania, personal correspondence 25 September 1995, 17 December 1998, 30 October 2006

Ineke Hania, interview in De Telegraaf 27 December 1994

Photograph & hand alphabet:
Ineke Hania

---

[2] Since 1 January 2009 Effatha has merged and is now part of Royal Dutch Kentalis, a large organization in the Netherlands for education and care for persons with hearing and speech disabilities.

AUSTRIA

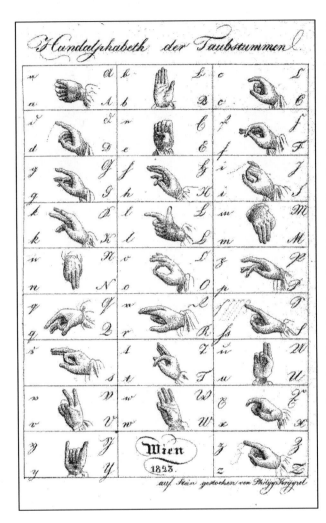

Figure 3: Austrian Hand Alphabet (1823)

In 1778, Empress Maria Theresa sent her son Joseph (who was to be crowned as Emperor Joseph II two years later) incognito to Paris to visit Marie Antoinette, her daughter, but also to look at the work of Abbé De l'Epée. One year later, the Empress sent the priest Johann Friedrich Stork, born in Aachen in 1746, and Joseph May, born on 5 January 1755 at Chabern in Leitmeritzer, to De l'Epée to learn how to teach deaf pupils. Stork and May returned to Vienna in 1779, where on 31 March 1779 an institute for the deaf was founded by Imperial Decree.

The school started with 12 pupils (six boys and six girls), who were selected to follow this education free of charge. They were informed about the school thanks to an imperial notice in the newspapers in Germany. Freiherr Hugo von Schütz, a deaf teacher from Germany, was also one of the pupils at the institute. On 22 December 1779, Stork gave his first public lesson, in the way De l'Epée usually did. Among the guests were crown prince Joseph, archduke Maximilian, and Cardinal De Migazzi. The subject was the bible story of the creation in Genesis. The pupils were also taught how to speak and make themselves properly understood. The next public lesson with a female student of high birth as the 'victim' took place on 19 January 1780 and was also very successful. From there on education for the deaf developed fast. By now, Stork and May had 23 pupils and a priest from Prague also visited to attend lessons.

The school received government support through structural subsidy and an annual salary for the teachers. They were allowed to use accommodation for teaching at the so called Bürgerspitall until 1782. The Emperor, now fully convinced of the importance of this kind of education, gave the institute a country house near Modling to maintain the finances of the Institute.

The decision to use the French method in Austria irritated the German teacher Samuel Heinicke. Stork remained as head of the school until 1790 and later wrote a book about his experiences: "Anleitung zum Unterricht Taubstummer nach der Lehrart des Herrn Abbé De l'Epée". He died in 1823. Over the years, Joseph May received much more recognition for his work as a teacher than Stork did. May had been the head of the institute from 1790 to 1819. He no longer slavishly followed the French method but rather a mixed Viennese method: written language, signs and a manual language for learning spoken language. May wrote a book: "Kurze Nachricht von der Verfassung und Einrichtung des Kaiserlich-Königlichen Taubstummen Instituts zu Wien, Ueber Taubstumme", Wien. He died in 1820.

Up to 1918, the year of the fall of the monarchy, the institute for the deaf was called the Imperial Deaf Institute, later it was renamed as the "Bundesinstitut für Gehörlosenbildung".

Figure 4: Deaf Institute in Vienna (1889)

Sources

Content:

Kruse, O.F., Ueber Taubstumme, Taubstummenbildung und Taubstummenanstalten; nebst Notizen aus meinem Reisetagebuche. Library number 990 Royal Dutch Kentalis. (Schleswig), 1853.

Leitner, Christiaan, personal correspondence 13 February 1991.

Schott, Walter, Das kaiserlich-königliche Taubstummen-Institut in Wien, eine Dokumentation. In: magazine Das Zeichen, nr. 35, March 1996 and letter, 14 February 1997.

Walther, Eduard, Geschichte des Taubstummen Bildungswesens. 144 – 146. Library number 1122 Royal Dutch Kentalis. (Wien), 1882.

Willer, Alfred, personal correspondence 7 July 1992.

Illustration:

Sechsunddreißigter Bericht vom Taubstummen Institutes In Wien vom 1889. Library number 1718 Royal Dutch Kentalis. (Wien), 1890.

Hand alphabet:

Austria-Hungary: Das Institut zu Wien, dessen Entstehung, Erweiterung und gegenwärtiger Zustand, by Michael Venus. Library number 1715 Royal Dutch Kentalis. (Wien), 1823.

BELGIUM

The Walloon Region

Still governed by William I, Sovereign of the Netherlands, Belgium at last gained stability as far as deaf education was concerned. A school for the deaf and the blind opened in Liège, thanks to the efforts of Jean-Baptiste Pouplin. This former officer was born in Gisors in France. Brother Orest wrote the following: "It happened on 2 June 1819. In a separate room, next to the classroom where in his capacity of a qualified teacher in Liège (Wallonia) he taught every day, Pouplin had assembled four deaf pupils. He was trying to teach them how to read and write, among other things by using an illustration of the hand alphabet for the deaf and dumb he chanced upon."

Pouplin was inspired by the example of the Groningen institute of the deaf of H.D. Guyot (their success of attracting donations and pupils). In March 1820, he made an appeal to benefactors and he continued to raise funds. In February 1822, the institute was founded and Pouplin became its director. Six months later, Joseph Henrion (1793-1868) was appointed as a deaf teacher to assist Pouplin, his father-in-law. Henrion was a former pupil of Sicard. He was born on 12 January 1793 at Verviers and died in 1868.

Figure 5: J.B. Pouplin

Figure 6: Canon Petrus Jozef Triest

Flemish region

Before special education for deaf pupils was available, canon Petrus Jozef Triest visited the French capital and also the oldest institute for the deaf in Paris. He also learnt that the Dutch King William I sympathized with the fate of handicapped people. It inspired him to act: in Ghent the Royal Institute for Deaf Girls was founded in 1820, run by the Sisters of Charity. The book "Kanunnik Triest" includes the following passage: "In 1819 canon Petrus Jozef Triest sent Miss Jeanne Verhulst, from Bruges, future Sister of Charity, to the national Institute for the Deaf and Dumb in Paris. The Reverend Salvan, one of the teachers at this institution, a friend of Mr. Triest, took Miss Verhulst under his wings. She stayed in Paris for nine months and returned to Ghent familiar with the teaching method for the deaf and dumb. Shortly afterwards, she entered the Congregation of the Sisters of Charity and with her entry received the name of Sister Vincentia. On 6 March 1820, the first girls were enrolled as pupils at the Terhaegen abbey and their number grew considerably."

A passage from the book "Kanunnik Triest, Stichter van de congregatie der Zusters van Liefde van Jezus en Maria. Zijn leven, zijn geest, zijn werken" reads as follows: "Monsignor Triest also felt a need to found a new school for deaf boys. He got in touch with William I, who was of the opinion that the Institute of Guyot was best suited to offer support. With the cooperation of the governor of East Flanders, canon Triest sent a request to William I to send a number of brothers at the expense of the state to Groningen, which took place on 7 April 1822. Under the supervision of the Dutchman Henri Daniel Guyot, Brother Aloïs Bourgois and

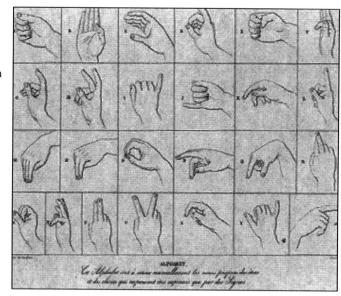

Figure 7: Belgian Hand Alphabet

Brother Xavier Cuyck were taught how to organize education for the deaf. In February 1825, these brothers were recalled to Ghent, although, according to H.D. Guyot, they had not yet completed their training. On 17 March 1825, they started with twelve pupils, the oldest being 31 years old. The institute was established in the Byloke building."

Sources

Content:

Anoniem, Kanunnik Triest (Brussel) 1926.

Baleine, Durup de, Institut Royal des Sourds-Muets et des Aveugles de Liège, notice historique, règlement, programmes et documents statistiques Library number 6693 of Royal Dutch Kentalis. (Liège) 1859.

Dierick, André, local history, personal correspondence. (Eksaarde, Belgium).

Orest, Brother, Studia Paedagogica Liber Amicorum Professor Dr. Victor d'Espaillier by broeder Orest, off print. (Leuven) without publishing year.

Pirenne, H., Geschiedenis in België (Gent) 1929, deel XII, 590.

Illustration:

J.B. Pouplin. Annuaire l'Institut Royale des Sourds-Muets, after page 45. Liège Library number 1526 of Royal Dutch Kentalis. (Liège), 1867.

Biographie de monsieur le chanoine P.J. Triest suivi d'une Statistique de tous les établissements qu'íl a fondés. Library number 610 Royal Dutch Kentalis. (Gand), 1836.

Hand alphabet:

In: 'Coup d'œil d; aveugles sur les sourds-muets' van Alexander Rodenbach. Library number 575 of Royal Dutch Kentalis. (Brussel), 1829.

BULGARIA

During the age-long suppression by the Ottoman (Turkish) empire, it was impossible to get anything done for the education of disabled persons and, also, deaf pupils. It was not until twenty years after the foundation of the Bulgarian state that it was possible to establish one or two care institutions.

The first school for the deaf was founded in Sofia in 1898 by Ferdinand Urbich, an acknowledged German teacher of the deaf. He was born in Kreutzburg on Vera in Germany. He completed his teacher's training in Eisenach and started his career in education teaching deaf pupils in Weimar, and afterwards in Hamburg for three years. He then taught a deaf boy in Heidelberg for eleven years. It was there that he met a number of Bulgarian students, Nicola Petkov from Vidin and Nicola Zlatin from Sofia.

Urbich asked them if Bulgaria already had a school for the deaf. They did not and Urbich felt it as his duty to do something for the deaf people in Bulgaria and thus he ended up in Sofia in 1897. He learnt to speak Bulgarian in one year.

Figure 8: Ferdinand Urbich

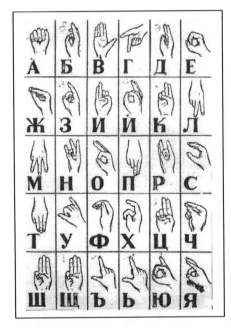

Figure 9: Bulgarian Hand Alphabet

In April 1898, he opened a private school for - probably - six pupils. His work there was successful and for eight years he paid for everything from his own pocket. In 1906, the government recognized Urbich's work and the school received the name: "the institute for the deaf recognized by the government". Ivan Shishmanov, the Minister of Education, was the initiator of this formal recognition. The public and the press were very supportive of Urbich's work and from time to time he received a government grant.

The method used by Urbich was the oral method, which he had brought with him from Germany. At the same time, he allowed deaf people to use gestures and mimics. He also took care of the training of new teachers for the deaf. He commanded so much respect that the Deaf Sports Club and a day nursery used his name.

He left Bulgaria in 1918 and lived in Germany until 1945.

Sources

Content & illustration:
Ivanov Venelin, personal correspondence 9 December 1992.

Hand alphabet:
O. Giaurov, Union of the Deaf in Bulgaria.

CROATIA

Adalbert Lampe was born deaf in Petrinja in 1842 and as in that time there was no school for the deaf in Croatia, his parents sent him to the Institution for the Deaf at Vienna. Lampe graduated with distinction, and at the institution learned the bookbinder's trade. After his return to his home, he worked as a civil servant and was eminently successful, because no such skilled bookbinder could be found in the whole neighborhood.

After a chance meeting with the mother of a deaf boy, named Ivan Smolec, she asked him to help her son. He gave up his business at Petrinja and moved to Agram, where, on account of his particularly fine handwriting, he secured a position as a clerk in the Provincial Government of Croatia.

Figure 10: School for the Deaf in Zagreb

Figure 11: Croatian Hand Alphabet

On 14 November 1885, he started as a private teacher in Agram (the former name of Zagreb) and obtained good results. This was the first time in Croatia that several deaf children were jointly instructed. In the annual report of 1888 it states that there no official papers of the foundation of the institute by Lampe are present. The deaf Institute was founded on 1 October 1888 with the name: "Privatinstitut Lampe".

Lampe used only sign language in his teaching. His school prospered because people really appreciated his attempts to prepare deaf pupils for society. In spite of this, Lampe initially did not receive any subsidy from the State. The pupils' parents had to pay sixteen forint per pupil, which was not enough to pay for food and heating. Therefore, Lampe kept his job as a civil servant. His wife took a job as a teacher and Lampe himself sometimes also taught in his spare time.

Until the year 1888, Lampe maintained his school solely by voluntary contributions. In that same year an association which aimed towards the foundation of an institution for the deaf in Croatia, undertook the management of the school, which shortly after started to expand and flourish.

On 26 of July 1891, Lampe conducted the last examination with his pupils, and resumed his duties as a clerk in the Government service, living in moderate circumstances till the day of his death on 19 July 1905 in Agram. Even when engaged in other duties, he never ceased to take a lively interest in the welfare of deaf people and in the Croatian Institution for the Deaf, which would hardly have sprung into existence without his zealous efforts in the beginning.

Sources:

Content:

Jelić, Sc. Slavica, personal correspondence October 2004.

Joseph Medved, Kroatien und Slawonien. In: Das Taubstummenbildungswesen im XIX. Jahrhundert in den wichtigsten Staaten Europas, ein Überblick über seine Entwicklung von Johannes Karth, 290–291.(Breslau), 1902, Found on 16 January 2013:
http://www.archive.org/stream/associationrevi04deafgoog/associationrevi04deafgoog_djvu.txt. In: The Association Review, 1906, 251 and 252.

Illustration:

Jelić, Sc. Slavica

Hand alphabet:

http://www.crodeafweb.net/rjecnik/abeceda/abeceda1.htm (last accessed on 31 January 2007)

CYPRUS

Figure 12: School for the Deaf in Nicosia

Nicosia, the capital of the Greek part of Cyprus, has a school for the deaf, which was founded in 1953 by George Markou, who today is called the "Father of deaf people."

In 1945, Semeli Tsatsou, head of the school for the deaf in Alexandria (Egypt), visited Cyprus as a tourist. During her time there, she spoke with someone from the Ministry of Education. She suggested that Cyprus should have a school for the deaf. The Ministry of Education passed on her suggestion to the Rotary Club of Nicosia. Within a year, the members collected the money needed for a scholarship, and in 1949 they sent George Markou to England to learn about the education for the deaf. The municipal administration of Nicosia offered a building to accommodate the school free of charge for a period of three years. The Ministry of Education also undertook the training of the necessary teaching staff.

Markou started the school for the deaf in Cyprus with 22 pupils, 16 of which were Greek and 6 Turkish. His two assistants were Greek and Turkish. In 1979, George Markou became the director of the school. From the very start of deaf education in Cyprus, the communication method never changed. The reasons for that being that the oral method had been used since the day of the school's inception, the majority of teachers prefer this method and had been accustomed to it since their training.

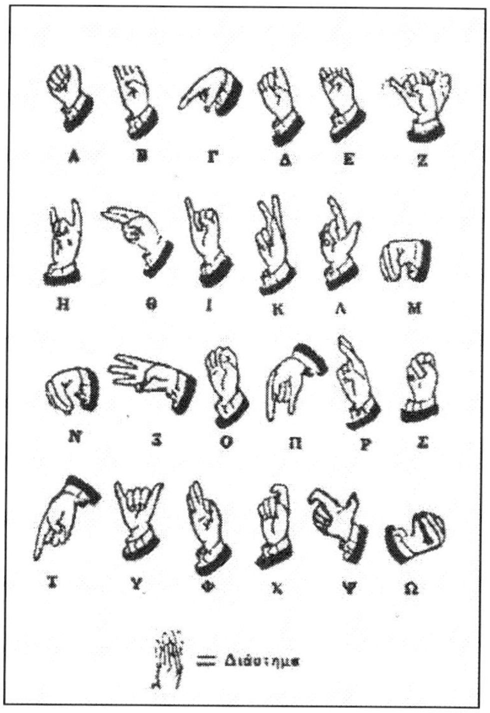

Sources

Content, illustration & hand alphabet:
Hadjkakou, Kika, (H.J.), personal correspondence July 2005.

Figure 13: Cyprus Hand Alphabet

CZECH REPUBLIC

The oldest Czech school for the deaf was founded in Prague in 1786 by the Freemason Lodge 'Seven Stars', also called the Scottish Brotherhood Kazimír. This institute founded the school for charitable reasons and therefore visited Emperor Joseph II to ask for advice. To their question which kind of charity would help them best, the Emperor replied that they should focus on deaf children. Until then, the monarchy had founded only one deaf school in Vienna.

The first teacher and headmaster of this school was Karl Berger. In 1767, he was ordained as a priest and worked as a chaplain in Schönfeld near Carlstadt. Even before 1780, he had already been involved with deaf children without education. Berger was so concerned with the fate of deaf children that in 1780 he decided to go to Vienna at his own expense. There, Stork taught him how to educate deaf children. In Platten, his home town, he taught deaf children in his own time. Circumstances forced him to give up this work.

In Prague, the freemasons were looking for a teacher and Karl Berger was regarded as a suitable candidate to lead the new institute and to teach there. He used finger spelling to teach reading and writing. If he wanted to explain a certain term, he used natural gestures and sometimes also sign language. He taught some of the pupils how to speak.

The school started with 6 pupils. Their names and ages were:

- Franz Aiger, 20 years old, son of a tailor from Prague;
- Johann Krimlak, 8 years old, from Ratenic on the Damenstiftsherrschaft Cerhenic;
- Karl Vocásek, 36 years old, shoemaker's assistant from Mies;
- Anna Lissauer, 12 years old, daughter of an officer from Prague;
- Katharina Renner, 26 years old, daughter of a horse trader from Platten;
- Maria Anna Hoffmann, 14 years old, daughter of a carpenter from Kupferberg.

Figure 14: School for the Deaf in Prague

Thanks to Emperor Joseph II, the government gave financial and moral support. On 12 September 1787, the Emperor also paid a personal visit to the institute. Berger died after a short illness. Later, the oral method was introduced at the school by Ondrej Schwarz, the new headmaster.

Initially, the school did not have its own building. The teachers and pupils regularly had to move from place to place. In 1902, they moved to a new building in Prague 5, the district called Smíchov. In 1918, however, the building was taken over by the government of the Czech Republic, which had been founded that year. In 1926, the school returned again to the building in Smíchov. It is still being used by the school today.

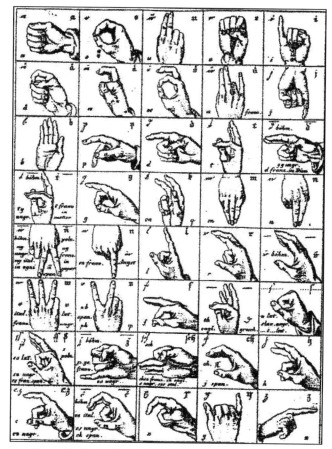

Figure 15: Czech Hand Alphabet

Sources:

Content:

Kmoch, Karl M., Beitrage zur Geschichte des Prager Privat-Taubstummen Institutes aus Anlass der Feier des 100-jährigen Bestehens desselben zusammengestellt. Library number 2717 of Royal Dutch Kentalis. (Praag), 1886

Novák, A., Gedenkschrift. (Praag), 1938.

Vlcková, Mária, personal correspondence, 22 May 1995.

Illustration:

Der Taubstummen-Privatinstitut. In: Die Medicinischen Anstalten Prag's, Prag, 1845. Library number 1704, before page 160 of Royal Dutch Kentalis.

Hand alphabet:

Czech, F.H., Versinnlichte Denk- und Sprachlehre, mit Anwendung auf die Religions- und Sittenlehre und auf das Leben. Library number 24 Royal Dutch Kentalis. (Wien), 1836.

DENMARK

The history of the Danish education for the deaf has two sources. The founder of the first school for the deaf, Georg Wilhelm Pfingsten, originated from what is now Germany. After the accession of King Christian from the house of Oldenburg (1448), Schleswig-Holstein, a small state, it fell to the Danish Crown. In 1864, this state became part of Prussia. After the assassination of Czar Peter III, Pfingsten cut short his stay in Saint Petersburg and returned to his country of birth. He was a keen music lover and sometimes worked as a music and dancing teacher. Fascinated by the movement of the human hands, he learnt the flag signaling system.

Figure 16: Peter Atke Castberg

In 1787, Pfingsten opened a school for the deaf in Lübeck (Schleswig-Holstein). He was supported financially by crown prince Frederic VI. Deaf children from poor families were able to receive an education thanks to state subsidy. Pfingsten taught his pupils how to communicate using the method of hand signals he had invented, which was also called "Schleswiger Schule". He also gave speech training.

In 1810, after the number of pupils had risen to 35, Pfingsten moved his school to Kiel. They were housed in a building which could easily hold 100 people. Helmut Vogel, a German deaf historian, wrote that since 1805 Margaretha Hüttmann worked at this school, first as an assistant and later as a teacher. Otto Friedrich Kruse also worked there since 1817 as a deaf teacher. He was a former pupil of the school and was taught the sign language by this lady.

The second source refers to Dr. Peter Atke Castberg[3] who founded a school for the deaf in Copenhagen in 1807. He was born in 1779 in Denmark of Norwegian parents. After his school years in Konigsberg, he moved to Copenhagen, where he studied medicine. He tried to cure deaf people by using galvanism (an experiment using current surges to restore residual hearing in deaf pupils). This caused a lot of pain but nobody was cured. Although it failed, the experiment convinced Castberg of the need to help deaf people, no matter how. Between 1803 and 1805, he looked around at schools for the deaf in Kiel, Berlin, Vienna and Paris. In this latter city he stayed for a while. He familiarized himself with the education for the deaf and also learnt from Sicard, a French abbé and teacher of the deaf, how to use the finger alphabet and manual gestures. After Castberg's return to Copenhagen, he wrote a recommendation letter to the government about the need to set up an institute for the deaf in Denmark. He argued for the need to protect deaf people, who until them had a negative image in society. Castberg wanted deaf people to become part of society through education. He did not wait for the government to reply but started a school which he personally financed. His pupils were a number of boys. Castberg taught them to use gestures and also the hand alphabet. These pupils also learnt how to speak and mimic. During a public 'examination' six months later, all the students passed. The same year, Castberg

[3] http://www.dovehistoriskselskab.dk/fileadmin/materialer/english/Folders/GB-Castberg.pdf (last accessed 24 April 2013)

published a book entitled "First Reader for a Deaf-Mute", and occasionally he would also hold lectures about Charles Michel de L'Epée.

On 17 April 1807, the crown prince of Denmark (who had taken over from his mentally ill father, King Christian VII) signed the deed of formation of the Danish institute for the deaf in Copenhagen. The Royal Family often attended the public 'examinations' of this institute. For several years, Castberg's education was very successful but in 1813 problems arose. Due to the war situation at the time, the Danish State, like many other countries, went bankrupt. This also meant the end of the annual state subsidy. In 1817, as the first country in the world, Denmark introduced compulsory school attendance for all deaf children. This led to a large influx of deaf pupils. Due to a lack of teachers, the school was unable to cope with these large numbers of students. Castberg died on 30 April 1823 in Copenhagen.

Figure 17: Danish Hand Alphabet

Sources

Content:

Emmerig, Ernst, Bilderatlas zur Geschichte der Taubstummenbildung. Library number 5530 Royal Dutch Kentalis. (München), 1927.

Biografieën in Dansk Biografisk Leksikon, part 18. (Kjöbenhavn), 1940.

Gudman, Sven, personal correspondence 15 September 1988.

Vogel, Helmut, personal correspondence September 2006.

Illustration:

Emmerig, Ernst, Bilderatlas zur Geschichte der Taubstummenbildung, 128. Library number 5530 Royal Dutch Kentalis. (München), 1927.

Hand alphabet:

Forelaesninger over Dövstumme Undervisningens Methode, holdne i Pastoralseminariet i Kjöbenhavn. Med Kobber over et Haandalfabet. Library number 1152 Royal Dutch Kentalis. (København), 1818.

ENGLAND

Early history

Figure 18: School for the Deaf in London

The first documented attempt to have a young deaf man accepted as a member of society is attributed to John Beverley, the bishop of Hexham, who was later canonized (he died in 712). He taught the young man how to speak. The Anglo-Saxon monk Beda 'Venerabilis' (The Venerable Bede) (672 or 673 – 735) mentioned it in his writing: "De Computo vel Loguela per Gestum Digitorum" (Counting or speaking with the fingers).

Peter Jackson (2004), a deaf author, wrote that in 1672 a testament was drawn up by one of two deaf brothers from a wealthy family in Norfolk entitled 'The will of Framlington Gaudy'. The parents had all their four sons, two of whom were hearing, educated. The two deaf brothers learnt how to write. On page 10 of his book, Jackson notes that literature exists about deaf education. The authors were William Holder (1615-1697) and John Wallis (1616-1703). The latter designed the typical English two-handed alphabet in 1652.

Classroom education

Thanks to the efforts of King George III, a private school called the "Academy" was founded in London in 1783. The teacher Thomas Braidwood (see the history of deaf education in Scotland) was offered 100 guineas if he was willing to set up the school in London. He complied with this request and he and his family moved to the opulent and leafy village of Hackney, now a borough in the east of London. Braidwood started with 12 pupils, all from rich families. In his teaching he used the mixed method, with the emphasis on language acquisition, reading and writing. The school relied on charity and did not receive any financial assistance from the State. Many students were from Great Britain and the British colonies in North America.

Joseph Watson, a nephew of Braidwood, came to help his uncle in 1784 and was regarded as a highly competent teacher. After his resignation in 1798, Braidwood remained closely associated with the education until the day he died. He was succeeded as head by his daughter Isabella. Thomas Arrowsmith, a former pupil, was later mentioned as a fairly good artist.

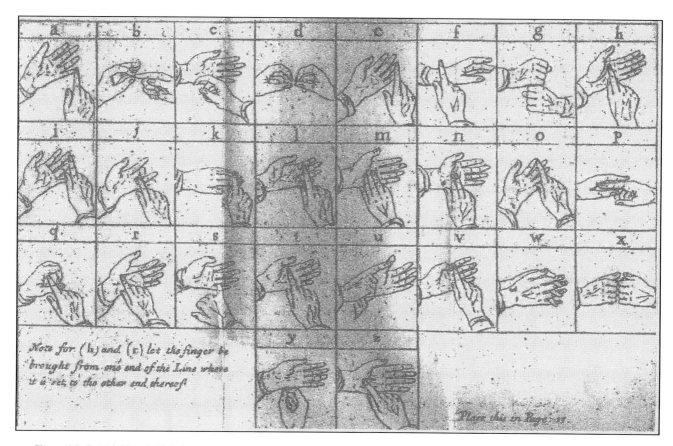

Figure 19: British Hand Alphabet

In 1792, a second (new) public school for the deaf was founded for children from poor families. This school was in Bermondsey, a borough in the east end of London. Until 1829, the head of this public school was Joseph Watson. The school used the oral method only.

Sources

Content:

Büchli, M.J.C., De zorg voor de doofstomme, 16 – 17. Library number 7868 of Royal Dutch Kentalis. (Amsterdam), 1948.

Hay, John and Lee, Raymond, Braidwood 1715 – 1806. In: Deaf History Journal, Vol. 1 Issue April, 1, 1997.

Hay, John, personal correspondence 28 August, 2005.

Jackson, Peter, Britain's Deaf Heritage. (Edinburgh), 1990

Lee, Raymond and Hay, John, Bermondsey 1792. (Feltham), 1993.

The Quarterly Review of Deaf-Mute Education, April 1887, vol. II, 167–173.

Watson, Joseph, Instruction of the Deaf and Dumb, xxvi – xxx. (London), 1809.

Illustration:

In: Historical sketch of the purposes, progress and present state of the asylum, Old Kent Road, with the rules of the society, 1824 - 1828, 1831, 1833, 1839, 1844. Library number 1551 of Royal Dutch Kentalis.(London), 1824.

Hand alphabet:

In: Digiti Lingua by Anonymous. (London), 1698.

ESTONIA

Early history

In 1903 Hörschelmann wrote: "The cradle of the Baltic education for the deaf was in Pernau. It was there that Jakob Wilde, professor, attached to the university of this town, taught deaf children in 1709 (this university later moved to Dorpat, now Tartu). This same year, because of the war, Wilde and other professors had to flee to Stockholm. It forced him to hand over the running of the school to Heinrich Niederhof (Nedderhow), pastor at Pernau." In a written statement in an inserted annex in Ammann's (1692) book (according to Mrs. Elle Ojasaar, this book is in possession of the Tartu university library), Niederhof wrote the following about speech education for deaf pupils: "On 12 March 1709, Jakob Wilde told me when he visited me that he had tried to familiarize himself with the contents of Ammann's speech education. After his departure, he left to me, Herrn Niederhof, pastor of the St. Nikolai Church, the contents of the deaf education." Unfortunately, the pastor died the same year. It is unknown how the education developed from then on till 1866 when the deaf school was founded.

Classroom teaching

Another source on education for the deaf in Estonia is Mrs. Ojasaar. For years she contributed articles on Estonian deaf education to the chronicle of the school for the deaf child in Porkuni. She worked for over 40 years as a teacher of deaf people.

Figure 20: Ernst Sokolovski

The official school for the deaf was founded on 23 December 1866 at Vändra in the southwest of Estonia (formerly known as Fennern). In 1866, the oral method was used and the language was, quite uniquely, Estonian. Unique, because at the time Estonia was a Russian province and the language of education at most schools was Russian or German. The founder of the school was Ernst Sokolovski, a Polish priest from Vändra, who was born in Latvia and died in Paldiski, an Estonian port to where he had been exiled by the Czarist regime.

The first teacher in Vändra was Johannes Eglon (1836-1908). He worked at the school for 33 years. Sokolovski was a man with a vision. He travelled across Europe to familiarize himself with the educational situation for deaf people. In his own church, he met several deaf children who were not receiving any education. In 1865, a rich landowner died and left 1000 roubles for education in

Estonia. Sokolovski tried to get a license to set up a school for the deaf. He tried to raise money by organizing collections in churches and in addition borrowed money. In 1866, a small house was built as a school for the deaf, which no longer exists today.

The Russian government did not support Estonian language teaching but it is not known whether they opposed it either. Due to the fact that Vändra was too far from the railway and the main roads, the school moved to a large country estate in Porkuni (Central Estonia). This was where on 5 January 1925 the current school for the deaf started with 9 pupils. Today, Estonia has two schools for the deaf and one school for children who are hard of hearing. One of these schools is in Tallinn (founded in 1994) and the other in Porkuni. The school for children who are hard of hearing is in Tartu.

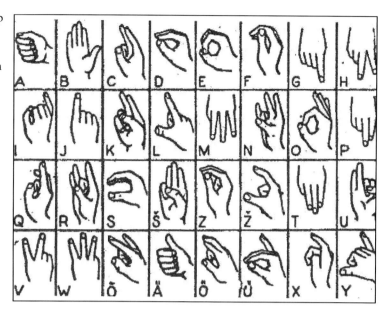

Figure 21: Estonian Hand Alphabet

Sources

Content:

Ammann, Joh. Conrad, Surdus loquens seu methodus qua, qui surdus natus est, loqui discere possit. (Amsterdam), 1692.

Hörschelmann, C., Uebersicht über das Werk der Taubstummenbildung mit besonderer Berücksichtigung der Anstalten in Russland. Library number 7164 of Royal Dutch Kentalis. (Tallinn), 1903.

Kannike, Ants, personal correspondence 31 August 1993.

Ojasaar, Elle, personal correspondence 18 April 1995.

Illustration & Hand alphabet:

Ojasaar, Elle

FINLAND

Porvoo, also known as Borgå, was the place where on 1 October 1846 Carl Oscar Malm gave his first private lessons to deaf pupils in Finland. The method he used was Swedish Sign Language and the hand alphabet and written Finnish.

Figure 22: Carl Oscar Malm

Malm was born in 1826 in Eura (Finland). The reason for Carl Oscar's deafness is not certain. Some say that it was a result of scabies, which Carl Oscar caught from his wet nurse[4]. During the illness, the boy's ears had been bleeding, and this was thought to have caused his deafness. A variety of methods had been used to try to cure it, including the application of electric current by a doctor in Stockholm, but without result.

When he was eight, Malm had to travel to Stockholm to a school for deaf pupils, the Manilla school. During his Swedish schooldays he learnt carpentry but his ambition was to be a teacher. At school, he was a very talented pupil and on his return to Porvoo he surprised his fellow citizens with his huge knowledge of languages: Finnish, Swedish, German, English, French and Swedish Sign Language. He would even sometimes have discussions with hearing intellectuals using pencil and paper.

After Malm started teaching two deaf boys at the Kankurinkuja no. 5 in Porvoo in 1846, several wealthy people helped him out financially. The local doctor gave him what he needed for free. Soon, Malm began to produce good results therefore it was no longer necessary to send deaf children from Finland to Sweden.

It took many years for Malm to prove himself before he received recognition from the State. Finally, in 1856, the school received financial support. In 1859, after searching for an ideal place for his school, the school finally moved to Abo (now Turku). His pupils went with him to Turku. Since no register was kept, or was lost, further statistical details about the pupils are lacking. One thing is certain: the names of only two pupils are known today: Sirén and Fritz Hirn. Fritz, who later married Maria Klingenberg, a photographer, became a famous photographer himself. Together with Malm, they searched for teaching material, which they tried to obtain by corresponding with people in Germany. In 1862, Fritz Hirn had his own studio, where he made photos of the signs of Finnish Sign Language, more than 300 in all.

It was said that the local shoemakers feared competition from deaf apprentice shoemakers in Turku, because of the excellent shoemaking skills they had acquired at the school. It was not until 1869 that the school was converted into the institute for the deaf.

---

4 http://www.kl-deaf.fi/Page/3b3c3115-afce-4ca7-999f-6ca74337a2ae.aspx (last accessed 24 April 2013)

Carl Oscar Malm also founded a national library in Turku. In his spare time he kept himself busy with his hobbies: chess, swimming and woodcraft. It was rumored in the deaf community that Malm and some others had saved a horse by pulling it out of the river. Malm caught a cold as a result and died at Turku at the age of 37.

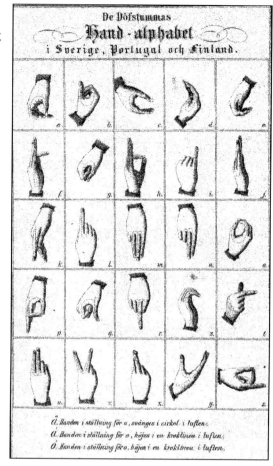

Figure 23: Finnish Hand Alphabet

Sources

Content:

Eerola, Riita, personal correspondence 20 September 1988.

Naukkarinen, Tiina, Fritz and Maria Hirn, Deaf Photographers. In: Collage, works on International Deaf History, by Renate Fischer and Tomas Vollhaber with the participation of Heiko Zienert, 104. Library number 7015 of Royal Dutch Kentalis. (Hamburg), 1996.

Salmi, Eeva, personal correspondence 18 October 2005.

Sayers, William. A Treatise from Enlightenment Sweden on Teaching the Mute to Read and Speak. In: Journal of Deaf Studies and Deaf Education, Fall 1999. http://www.kl-deaf.fi/Page/3b3c3115-afce-4ca7-999f-6ca74337a2ae.aspx (Last accessed April 2013)

Illustration:

Finnish museum of the Deaf: http://www.kl-deaf.fi/Page/3b3c3115-afce-4ca7-999f-6ca74337a2ae.aspx (last accessed 17 July 2013).

Hand alphabet:

Borg, E., Om Institutet för döfstumma och blinda. 1. Library number 1736 Royal Dutch Kentalis. (Stockholm), 1854.

FRANCE

Early history

The first speech teacher was Jacobo Rodríguez Pereira, born on 11 April 1715 at Berlanga (Portugal). Between 1734 and 1780 he taught twelve students how to speak using a hand alphabet based on phonetic principles. Like Samuel Heinicke's, Pereira's teaching method was surrounded by secrecy. His best known pupils were Etienne de Fay, a child from a wealthy family and Sabourex de Fontaney, godson of duce De Chaulnes, who later wrote in his autobiography about the speech method used by his instructor.

Etienne de Fay (1669 – 1746 or 1747), who was born deaf, lived in a monastery and worked as a sculptor on the cathedral of Amiens. He also worked as an architect, librarian, and teacher of a number of deaf pupils.

In those days, Pereira competed with Monsieur Ernaud, who also used Johann Conrad Ammann's book as a basis for his speech instruction. One of Ernaud's pupils was the son of an Irish nobleman who was born deaf. After his death in 1780, he was succeeded by Isaac, his son, but his attempts to complete the work of his father failed miserably and he died young survived by his mother and wife with two young children.

Classroom teaching

The world's first school for the deaf with whole-class teaching was founded by Abbé Charles Michel de l'Epée in 1760. In the same year, a similar school started in Scotland (Thomas Braidwood) but this cannot be classified as classroom teaching.

Figure 24: Abbé Charles Michel de l'Epée

De l'Epée was born in Versailles on 24 November 1712, and was raised by his parents at a stone's throw distance from the Royal Palace of Louis XIV, the Sun King. His father was employed at this palace as a royal architect. His job included maintaining the buildings. When Charles Michel was seven years old, the family moved to the center of Paris. From his early childhood he wanted to be a priest. He studied at the Palais Royale, the center of the Jansenism (a theological movement in Roman Catholicism, founded by the Dutchman Cornelis Jansen). In 1728, De l'Epée followed a course in philosophy; two years later he registered as a student at the Sorbonne.

In 1760, he met deaf twins at their house in the rue Fossées des Saint Victor (now: rues Thouin et du Cardinale Lemoine). He saw how the twin sisters used finger spelling to communicate with each other. Their mother told him that the girls could only communicate with the hands and she asked the 47-year old priest if he knew anyone who could teach them. The girls turned out to be pupils of Simon Vanin (1704 Reims – 1759 Paris), a priest who had died shortly before. It meant that they had lost their teacher. This made a deep impression on the abbot. He tried to find a teacher for the girls but he could not find anyone. It suddenly dawned upon de l'Epée that the girls might die without knowing about the important things of life, such as marriage and bringing up children.

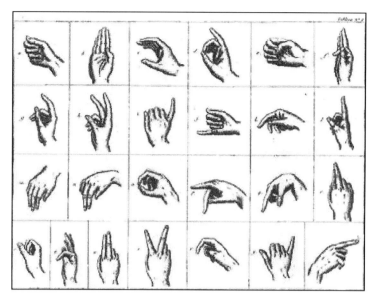

Figure 25: French Hand Alphabet

After his decision to take a plunge himself, the twins visited the priest at his home several times a week to be educated. After a while, he noticed that there was a real need for this kind of teaching because word of mouth spread and soon he received a request from some parents to teach their deaf children. He received the unconditional support from his brother and sister, who were only able to help him with material matters. People gradually got to know about his work, also abroad.

One day, he got hold of a wonderful book written by Juan Pablo Bonet, published in 1620 in Spain. De l'Epée's interest was aroused when he saw the beautiful illustrations of the hand alphabet. Later, De l'Epée received or bought another book written by Johann Conrad Ammann from Amsterdam. He later said that these two books were a guide for his teaching. Later, De l'Epée also received an envelope with a royal seal from Empress Catherine the Great of Russia. She asked him to come to Russia immediately to teach deaf children. De l'Epée, already getting on in years, did not fancy the idea and sent a compatriot instead.

A count of Frankenstein, the son of Empress Thèrese of Austria, visited Paris incognito and also dropped in at De l'Epée's school to watch his teaching. He was so impressed by what he saw that he asked De l'Epée to travel to Austria and set up a school for the deaf there. This made De l'Epée realize that schools for the deaf were also needed in other countries. He asked the crown prince to send an available teacher from Austria to Paris so that De l'Epée could teach him the ropes. He thus acquired his first two hearing apprentices: Friedrich Stork, a priest, and Josef May, an old-soldier and teacher.

One day De l'Epée decided to invite the general public to come and watch him work as a teacher. He subsequently held a public lesson once a week. In those days, this was something completely new. The hearing audience saw the pupils make strange hand movements and of course did not understand how they were able to express themselves in this way. Before 1760, deaf people did not receive any education at all and were excluded from society. By being allowed to attend these public lessons, hearing people could see for themselves that deaf people were not useless creatures but fellow citizens. As a gesture of goodwill people supported his education financially although it was not nearly enough.

From 1780 onwards, a total of seventeen clergymen from all over Europe served their apprenticeships with De l'Epée. Afterwards they returned to their own countries, with all the knowledge they needed to set up deaf schools at home. There were also some who had the intention to do so but eventually did not.

The priest and teacher Charles Michel de l'Epée died at the age of 77 amidst his pupils and a number of hearing friends two days before Christmas of that year. He was buried in a church (Saint Roch) in the center of Paris. His ideal to provide education to deaf children all over the world continues to live on.

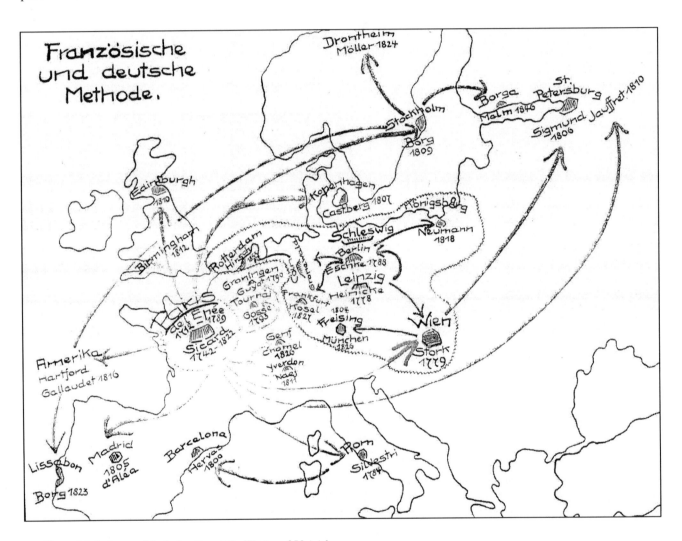

Figure 26: Influence of deaf education of De l'Epée and Heinicke

Sources

Content:

Bender, Ruth E., The conquest of deafness. Library number 3509 Royal Dutch Kentalis. (Cleveland 6, Ohio, USA), 1960.

Bézagu-Deluy, Maryse, L'abbé de L'Epée, instituteur gratuit des sourds et muets 1712 – 1789. Library number 6087 Royal Dutch Kentalis. (Paris), 1990.

Büchli, M.J.C., De zorg voor de doofstomme. Library number 7868 Royal Dutch Kentalis. (Amsterdam) 1948.

Truffaut, Bernard, articles. In: Cahiers de l'Histoire des Sourds. (St. Jean de la Ruelle), 1989.

Illustrations:

Illustration of Abbé C.M. de l'Epée, owned by Henk Betten.

Drawing. In: Bilderatlas zur Geschichte der Taubstummenbildung by Ernst Emmerig. Library number 5530 Royal Dutch Kentalis. (München), 1927.

Hand alphabet:

In: Cours d'instruction d'un sourd-muet de naissance, pour servir a l'éducation des sourds-muets by Roch Ambroise Sicard, Paris Chez le Clere, 1799. Library number 587-S bis, Royal Dutch Kentalis. (Hamburg), 1799.

GERMANY

Early history

The earliest attempts to teach deaf people how to speak can be read in a book written by Emmerig. He wrote about Joachim Pascha (1527-1578), who as a preacher at the court of Joachim II, the Elector of Brandenburg, gained his reputation with the book "Küster in der Neuausgabe der 1670 u. 1671 erschienen Bildersammlung". (M. Fr. Seidel, Berlin, 1751). He had eight children, one of which, his daughter Elisabeth, was deaf. He taught her how to make gestures with the aid of pictures and as such he is seen by some as the precursor of Simon Vanin, who taught deaf twin sisters until 1759 in Paris.

Figure 27: Deaf Institute in Leipzig

In 1718, G. Raphel produced a book entitled, "Die Kunst, Taube und Stumme reden zu lernen...," in which he wrote about his experiences as a teacher of his own deaf daughter. Raphel used the works of Ammann as a model.

Figure 28: Samuel Heinicke

Classroom teaching

The institute for the deaf in Leipzig was founded on 14 April 1778. The Samuel Heinicke School was to be the 'erste staatliche Taubstummenanstalt der Welt'[5]. Samuel Heinicke was born in Nautschütz near Weissenfels and died in Leipzig. While looking for a supplementary income, he read the book by Ammann. In his own book, which he wrote in Eppendorf near Hamburg, he relates how he got to know a deaf boy. At the request of the boy's father, Heinicke took him on as his pupil in 1754. Encouraged by his success, 20 years later the number of pupils had grown to five. Thanks to a man named Schröder, a captain in the Saxon army, who attended a public lesson, Heinicke's work came to the attention of Friedrich August, the Elector of Saxony. He asked him to move his school to Leipzig where he would

---

[5] http://www.xn--landesschule-fr-hrgeschdigte-snc74c1f.sachsen.de/ (last accessed 24 April 2013)

earn a princely salary. Heinicke did so, and took his pupils, which numbered nine by then, with him. However, several professors of the University of Leipzig resisted this move. Probably because they could not abide seeing someone with Heinicke's background gain such prominence: he had been a mere soldier and did not have the qualifications to teach. Later, he also faced obstruction from the city of Leipzig but despite his limited financial resources Heinicke continued to teach. He had to, just to escape the poverty which many people had to endure because of the war that was going on. Besides teaching his oral method, Heinicke also used writing and sometimes sign language, purely as an aid.

Figure 29: German Hand Alphabet

Sources

Content:

Ammann, Joh. Conrad, Redende Taube oder Abhandlung von der Sprache. (Dresden und Leipzig), 1747.

Emmerig, Ernst, Bilderatlas zur Geschichte der Taubstummenbildung. Library number 5530 Royal Dutch Kentalis. (München), 1927.

Karth, J., Das Taubstummenbildungswesen im XIX. Jahrhundert in den wichtigsten Staaten Europas. Library number 2365 Royal Dutch Kentalis. (Breslau), 1902.

Walther, Eduard, Geschichte des Taubstummen-Bildungswesens. Library number 1122 Royal Dutch Kentalis. (Bielefeld und Leipzig), 1882.

Illustration:

Dresden; Sächsische Landesbibliothek - Staats–und Universitätsbibliothek Dresden. Gustav Frank lith. - [S.l.] , ab 1856. (Dresden), 1856.

Emmerig, Ernst, Bilderatlas zur Geschichte der Taubstummenbildung. Library number 5530 Royal Dutch Kentalis (München), 1927.

Hand alphabet:

Anleitung, taubstumme Kinder im Schreiben, Lesen, Rechnen und Reden zu unterrichten usw. Mit einer Abbildung des Handalphabets. Library number 836 Royal Dutch Kentalis. (Gmünd), 1821.

GREECE

Early history

Aristotle and Plato were already concerned with deafness. Büchli (1948) wrote: "Aristotle points to the importance of the tongue for speech and to the fact that small children need to learn to use their tongue. As long as they are not able to control it, they will not speak well. Aristotle believed that blind people are more receptive to development than deaf people, because hearing is more conducive to intellectual development; through (audible) speech knowledge is imparted in education. One can reconcile oneself with this argument but later these passages were incorrectly interpreted. The allegation that without hearing it was impossible to be educated was attributed to Aristotle. For deaf people this has the disastrous consequence that theologians and jurists citing Aristotle denied deaf people intellectual development."

"Plato was the first to mention possibilities for deaf people to develop: in a dialogue with Socrates about the relationship between word and understanding Plato refers to the deaf who made themselves understood by using sign language." (Büchli, 1948; p. 14).

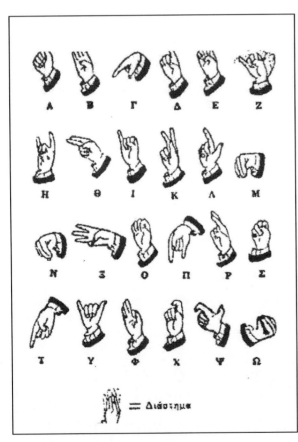

Figure 30: Greek Hand Alphabet

Classroom teaching

Oddly enough, it was not until the first quarter of the 20th century that deaf education was introduced in Greece. It started with the benefactor Charalambos Speliopoulos who wanted to set up a National Institute for the Deaf as early as 1907 but for various reasons nothing came of it. He intended to name the school for the deaf: "House of Charalambos and Helen (his wife) Speliopoulos". This wealthy man died in 1922.

In 1922, a ship with Greek refugees from Turkey arrived at the port of Athens. On board, there were also orphans, some of whom were deaf. The American charity "Near-East Foundation" helped orphans, also deaf children. Helen Palatidou, a refugee herself, was sent in the early twenties to America to learn how to educate deaf children. She stayed for about two years. When she returned, she immediately started teaching ten pupils in Athens, supervised by this charity. They also ran an orphanage for deaf children, on the island of Syros.

The teaching method used was the oral method. It was not until 1931 that the government, through the Ministry of Health, set up a charity for deaf children. One year later, the board of this institute, called "House of the Deaf by Charalambos Speliopoulos", managed to merge two institutes, a public and a private school, by a special law. It was not until 1937 that the school received the status of "National Institute for the Protection of the Deaf", which also received new and larger accommodation from the Ministry.

Sources

Content:

Büchli, M.J.C., De zorg voor de doofstomme, 16 – 17. Library number 7868 Royal Dutch Kentalis. (Amsterdam), 1948.

Fitsiou, A., personal correspondence, 20 May 1991.

Hadjkakou, Kika, (H.J.), personal correspondence July 2005.

Lampropoulou, Venetta, The History of Deaf Education in Greece In: The Deaf Way, perspectives from the International Conference on Deaf Culture (Gallaudet University Press), 1994.

Hand alphabet:
Kika, (H.J.) Hadjkakou.

HUNGARY

The town of Vac, to the north of Budapest, was the place where on 15 August 1802 a school for deaf students was founded. Mr. András Jólészi Cházár, who was born at Jólész and died at Rozsnyó, resigned his position as a lawyer because of his advanced age and devoted himself to helping poor and disabled people. After he had visited the Viennese institute for the deaf, he founded an institute for the deaf in his own country. He himself contributed ƒ 1000 (Österreichisch-Ungarischer Gulden) and collected another ƒ 40,000 to give the school a new lease of life.

Figure 31: András Jólészi Cházár

The first head of the new institute was Anton Simon (1772 - 1808), a priest. He was the real professional they were looking for and he wrote two books about his time in Vac, one in 1804, and a second called *A True Master* in 1807. He managed to teach his pupils to read and write in a short time.

Anton Schwarzer and Samuel Kapuváry assisted Anton Simon as teachers. They used the mixed Viennese method but the language the pupils were taught to speak was partly German and partly Hungarian. This school started with 24 pupils who were between 7 and 14 years old. They also learnt a trade. The institute received moral and financial support from the Empire. King Franz I of Hungary donated ƒ 5000 and allowed them to use the vacant Episcopal palace. Structural subsidies were also received from all kinds of funds.

Figure 32: Hungarian Hand Alphabet

In 1878, an institute for deaf Jewish students was opened in the same building. The first director of this new institute, Lipot Grunberger, used the oral method.

Sources

Content:

Toth, Egon, personal correspondence, 3 January 1997.

Schott, Walter, personal correspondence, 13 February 1997.

Emmerig, Ernst, Bilderatlas zur Geschichte der Taubstummenbildung. Library number 5530 Royal Dutch Kentalis. (München), 1927.

Varadi, S., Ungarn. In: Das Taubstummenbildungswesen im XIX. Jahrhundert in den wichtigsten Staaten Europas by J. Karth, Library number 2365 Royal Dutch Kentalis (Breslau), 1902.

Illustration:

In: Bilderatlas zur Geschichte der Taubstummenbildung by Ernst Emmerig, p. 199., (München), 1927.

Hand alphabet:

Lehrmethode zum Unterricht der Taubstummen in der Tonsprache für Lehrer by Anton Schwarzer, after 518. Royal Dutch Kentalis Library number 1077. (Waitzen), 1828.

ICELAND

Figure 33: Páll Séra Pálsson

Páll Séra Pálsson, a priest, started to teach deaf pupils in 1870 at his home "Stóra Hraun" on the south coast of Iceland. The method used was the Danish gestural method. Later, they used the mixed method: speech and gestural communication.

On 26 February 1872, the Danish government finally gave this private school a status but it was not until twenty years later, on 1 October 1892, that the institute for the deaf was founded. In 1909, the institute moved to Reykjavik. It was called: "Heyrnleysingjaskólinn". In 1993, the school had a total of 25 pupils from 6 to 15 years old. The language used is Icelandic and sign language.

Camilla Mirja Björnsdóttir, a deaf woman from Iceland, provided the following information: between 1820 and 1867, 24 deaf pupils, all born in Iceland, were sent to Denmark to enroll in education (from 1814 to 1944 Iceland was under the Danish crown). Due to the large distance, these pupils hardly had any holidays.

Pálsson was born hearing. When he was very young he had only a very limited vocabulary. Therefore, he was also sent to a school for the deaf in Denmark. There, he hugely expanded his vocabulary. It is not known how long he stayed there. He returned to his own country and founded a Latin school and seminary. He worked from his father's house. In 1865/66, he lost his job and started to write very simple schoolbooks for deaf pupils.

On 4 September 1867, he started to teach deaf pupils. We do not know what method Pálsson used for his instruction. According to a note in a letter that was found, he definitely used sign language. This school was initially located in Prestbakki but in 1878 Pálsson moved the school to Skaftafell. During his life, he only taught four pupils. When they had learnt enough, they worked as valets or home helps.

Since Pálsson requested the Danish government to introduce compulsory education for deaf children in Iceland but his request was turned down. Compulsory education was not introduced in Iceland until 1922. This was quite odd because Denmark itself had introduced compulsory education for

Figure 34: School for the Deaf in Reykjavik

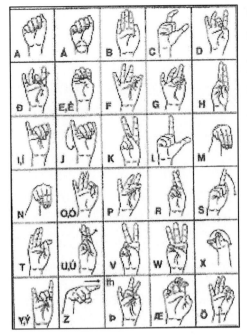

Figure 35: Icelandic Hand Alphabet

deaf children by Royal Decree. After the death of Páll Séra Pálsson, subsidy started to trickle in, enabling the school to take on more pupils.

In 2003, a group of deaf pupils were integrated into mainstream primary education. This group consisted of 18 pupils, some of which were hard of hearing.

Sources

Content:

Björnsdóttir, Camilla Mirja, personal correspondence, August 2003.

Gudjón Indridason, personal correspondence 13 August 2013.

Njálsdóttir, Bjarney, personal correspondence, 30 September 1993.

Illustration:
Gudjón Indridason, personal photograph.

Hand alphabet:
In: International Hand Alphabet Charts, second edition, edited and compiled by Simon J. Carmel. (Rockville, Md, USA), 1982.

IRELAND

Around 1812, a gentleman with the name of Robinson approached the government about setting up a national institute for the deaf after the example of the work of Sicard in Paris. Unfortunately, the government was not even prepared to discuss his proposal and Robinson gave up his attempts to try and convince the government.

Four years later, on 18 May 1816, the first institute for the deaf in Ireland was founded. According to the annual report

Figure 36: National Institution for Deaf & Dumb of the Poor, Claremont, Ireland

of 1817, the official name of this institute was the National Institution for the Education of Deaf and Dumb Children of the Poor in Ireland.

Dr. Charles Orpen, protestant and surgeon, met Thomas Collins, a deaf boy, in a hospital and tried to teach him speech and general knowledge at his own home. Following this success, Orpen held several lectures at the hospital in 1816, which were also attended by Thomas as a textbook example. This led to the foundation of the protestant institute. The methods used were said to be those of speech and mimicking mouth movements but it is known that Orpen was a convinced adherent of the manual method of Abbé De L'Epée and Sicard. The methods referred to by Orpen in his book, are the One-Handed or Spanish Manual Alphabet and Two-Handed or English Manual Alphabet were both used at the school.

In 1817, a committee rented a house paid for by the House of Industry in the Brunswick Street in Claremont near Glasnevin, now a district of Dublin. It offered much more space to teach 16 pupils. In 1822, the institute added several new classrooms and a boarding school to the school. They also employed deaf teachers. Like other institutes for the deaf, this institute also switched to the oral system in 1880.

Catholic parents were not very happy with the 'indoctrination' that pupils were exposed to at the institute. Given its dependence on donations, the institute became a Catholic school in 1840.

Charles Edward Herbert Orpen was born in Cork and married Alicia Frances Sirr in 1823. Charles was her second husband. They had 9 children. In 1848, they immigrated to South Africa, where Charles worked as a pastor for eight years and where he died in Port Elizabeth. By 1844, the number of pupils reached 136, prior to the establishment of the Catholic Institution for the Deaf and Dumb in Cabra (St Mary's for Girls – 1846 and St Joseph's for Boys - 1857).

Figure 38: Irish Hand Alphabet, one handed

Figure 37: Irish Hand Alphabet, two handed

Sources

Content:

Gawley, J., personal correspondence, 18 July 1988.

Irish Deaf History: http://www.irishdeafhistory.com/story.html

Illustration:

Orpen, Ch. E.H., The contrast between atheism, paganism and christianity; illustrated; or the uneducated deaf and dumb, as heathens, compared with those, who have been instructed in language and revelation, and taught by the holy spirit, as Christians. Library number 673 Royal Dutch Kentalis. (Dublin, 1827).

Hand Alphabet:

Orpen, Ch. E.H., Anecdotes and Annals of the Deaf and Dumb. Library number 674 Royal Dutch Kentalis. (London), 1836.

ITALY

Early history

Carl Mander (1604) wrote: "Quintus Pedius, who had been the mayor of Rome, and had publicly triumphed in Rome, who with Emperor August was a co-heir of Julius Caesar, had a son, whose name also was Quintus Pedius. As this boy was born dumb, the parents consulted on what he should be taught. Messala (…) believed and advised after long consideration and serious thought that they should teach this dumb boy the art of painting, which advice the Emperor August took to heart. And thus this young dumb boy continued with this art until his death and he was a very capable artist too."

"Hieronymus Cardanus (1501-1576), physician, distinguished in 1550 between people who were born deaf or became deaf shortly after birth, and those who were able to speak when they became deaf. The former, provided they had the power of reason, could develop normally, as he knew from experience. In a later writing – with reference to Agricola – he emphasized that they were equally capable to denote concrete and abstract concepts both in writing and orally, as the deaf and dumb do." (Büchli, 1948).

Classroom teaching

In 1782, deaf children in Italy did not receive any education, which was something that bothered Pasquale di Pietro, a wealthy lawyer. He decided to set up, at his own expense, a school for the deaf in Rome. A year earlier, he visited the school for the deaf of Abbé De l'Epée in Paris. Back in Rome, he met Tommasso Silvestri, a priest, and sent him to the school in Paris to master the skills needed for this kind of education. Silvestri needed six months before he was able to use the sign language and the hand alphabet. On 9 February 1784, he started with eight pupils in Pasquale di Pietro's house. He was so successful with his attempts to teach his pupils to speak that he was visited by various people from Naples, Malta, Modena and other places who wanted to learn his method. Later, Silvestri described his method in his unpublished book, the title of which translates as: 'A fast method for teaching and instructing, intended for teachers of deaf and dumb children, who are born this way'. Silvestri taught for five more years and died in 1789 at a young age.

Figure 39: Tommasso Silvestri

From its earliest days, the school found favor with the Pope thanks to the efforts of Pasquale di Pietro, and it also received financial support.

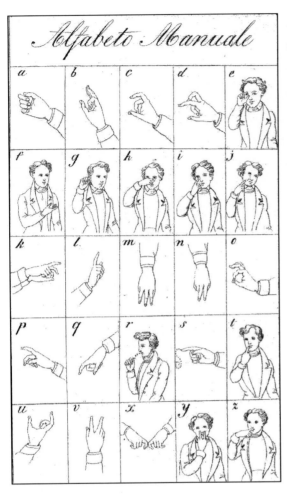

Figure 40: Italian Hand Alphabet

After Silvestri's death, the school met with adversity and resistance, one of the reasons being that Mariani, di Pietro's successor, had absolutely no experience with education for the deaf but he, nonetheless, remained the director for 42 years. The school also attracted pupils from small provinces, such as Piedmont, Tuscany, Stato Pontificio, Regno di Napoli and others. These provinces also financed the school.

It is hard to tell how many schools for the deaf there currently are in Italy, because deaf children are nearly always integrated into mainstream education. One thing is certain: in 1800 there were two schools for the deaf, in 1850 there were seventeen and in 1900 Italy had 47 schools for the deaf.

Sources

Content:

Büchli, M.J.C., De zorg voor de doofstomme,15 (Amsterdam), 1948.

Cimino, Enrico, October, personal correspondence, 31th, 1996.

Don Tommaso Silvestri, de Italiaansche Abbé de l'Epée en de eerste die de doofstommen leerde spreken. In: Algemeen Nederlands Doven Orgaan, August 1934. (translation of La Gazette des S.-M., Paris by Louis Monasch Jr.)

Emmerig, Ernst, Bilderatlas zur Geschichte der Taubstummenbildung Library number 5530 Royal Dutch Kentalis. (München),1927

Mander, Carl van, Het schilderboeck: waer in voor eerst de leerlustighe iueght den grondt der edel vry schilderconst in verscheyden deelen wort voorghedraghen. (Haarlem), 1604.

Pinna, Paola, L. Pagliari Rampelli, P. Rossini, V. Volterra, Written and unwritten History of a Resídidential School for the Deaf in Rome, 349–368. In: Looking Back, A Reader on the History of Deaf Communities and their Sign Languages, by Renate Fischer and Harlan Lane (eds.) Library number 6106 Royal Dutch Kentalis. (Hamburg), 1993.

Illustration:

Donnino, Alfonso Girolamo, L'arte di far parlare i sordomuti dalla nascita e l'abbate Tommaso Silvestri: memorie. Library number 1912 Royal Dutch Kentalis. (Armanni) 1889.

Hand alphabet:

Pendola, Tommaso, Di pratico insegnamento per il sordo-muto Italiano. Library number 388, Royal Dutch Kentalis. (Siena, 1842).

LATVIA

In 1809 Carl August Jakobi started working as a private teacher for six deaf pupils in Riga. The age for admission was 6 to 12. The subjects the pupils were taught were writing, arithmetic, drawing, religion, language, biology, geography, and history. The pupils also learnt how to speak and read. The teaching method used was initially the manual method. Older students were also taught handicrafts: stone-cutting, wood-turning, and paper cutting. Later, students also learnt how to make a seal. The course at this school lasted 4 to 5 years.

In 1832, a deaf man, Daniël Heinrich Senß, born in Potsdam, former pupil of the institute for the deaf in Berlin, wanted to set up a second private school in Riga. On 25 January of that year, he started with 6 pupils funded by Dr. Ph. Bornhaupt. The school lasted only one year.

Senß used the manual method. Pastor Taube gave speech lessons. The deaf son of the widow of major Ehlert, who was a pupil at this school, later became a teacher at a school for the deaf.

Eight years later, the new "Anstalt der Literärisch-praktische Bürgerverbindung zu Riga" was founded. In 1845, a Mr. Berg from Berlin was appointed as a teacher at a salary of 400 roubles a year. Meanwhile, Ehlert, the former deaf pupil, tried to set up a private institute; he was a good teacher but was opposed to the German method because he preferred hand gestures. He worked as a teacher until 1866.

After the number of pupils had dropped to five, the deplorable condition of this institute, which had lasted for years, finally ended thanks to the efforts of a new employee, Stünzi from Riehen (Switzerland). Until Stünzi's death, the institute prospered. This led the board of the "Anstalt der Litterärisch-praktische Bürgerverbindung zu Riga" to remark that: "The name of Stünzi will have pride of place in the history of schools for the deaf and dumb in the Baltic States, and later generations will definitely remember the deceased with gratitude and respect."

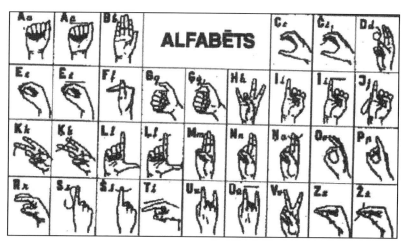

Figure 41: Latvian Hand Alphabet

Sources

Content:

Hörschelmann, C., Uebersicht über das Werk der Taubstummen-bildung met besonderer Berücksichtigung der Anstalten in Russland. Library number 7164 Royal Dutch Kentalis (Tallinn), 1903.

Karth, J., Das Taubstummenbildungswesen im XIX. Jahrhundert in den wichtigsten Staaten Europas. Library number 2365 Royal Dutch Kentalis (Breslau), 1902

Kruse, O.F., Ueber Taubstumme, Taubstummenbildung und Taubstummenanstalten; nebst Notizen aus meinem Reisetagebuche Library number 990 Royal Dutch Kentalis (Schleswig), 1853.

Zigmunde, Alīda. Die Entwicklung der Gehörlosenbildung in Lettland von den Anfängen in Livland und in Kurland bis zur Gegenwart, 157. (Riga), 2011.

Hand alphabet:

Edgar Volslovs, personal correspondence, May 2005.

LITHUANIA

In a letter, Daiva Burkauskiene, teacher of Vilnius Deaf Boarding School, writes: "I cannot refrain from telling you that Anzelmas Zigmantas, a monk, started with the education as early 1805. He gave private lessons. This acted as an inspiration for Jonas Kosakovskis, bishop of Vilnius, and in 1806 he proposed to have an institute for the deaf established in the capital of Lithuania. Before he was able to realize this plan, he died. It should also be mentioned that this education was interrupted because of the war of 1812."

It was not until 1833 before the first school was opened in Vilnius thanks to the efforts of a charity, a project of the local university. Karolis Malochovecas, a teacher, had four deaf pupils. He used the manual method but the curriculum also included speech, which was taught to gifted pupils. How the first Lithuanian teachers learnt sign language is not known.

Acquiring the necessary funding for the school was not easy in those days. Since Lithuania was part of the Russian Empire at the time, they asked the government for funding but it was turned down. Fortunately, there was a fund in the name of Jonas Kosakovskis, bishop of Vilnius, from which they could occasionally draw.

Sources

Content:
Burkauskiene, Daiva, personal correspondence, 14 May 1999.

Hand alphabet:
Arunas Brazinskas, personal correspondence, September 2006.

Figure 42: Lithuanian Hand Alphabet

LUXEMBOURG

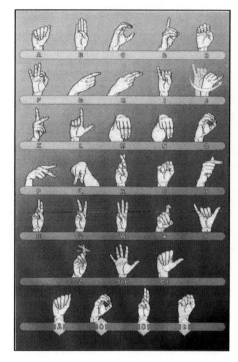

Figure 43: Luxembourg Hand Alphabet

From 1844 to 1880, deaf pupils were generally taught at the institute for the deaf in Bad Camberg (Germany). Some previously also attended the institute at Metz.

The government decided to set up a new institute in the city of Luxemburg. As director-general of the Ministry of Education, Mr. H. Kirpach (1841-1913) was asked to take care of matters and drew up several articles of the Royal Decree. This Decree was signed in The Hague on 28 January 1880 by King William III of the Netherlands (until 1890, Luxemburg was part of the Kingdom of the Netherlands).

In that year, there were 38 pupils of school age and the teachers were J. Kimmes from Remich and Joseph Schuller from Vianden. They worked at the school until respectively 1909 and 1922. Two years later they were joined by Nicolas Hemmen, who stayed on till 1923. Instruction was according to the oral method. The government supported this education both morally and financially.

Since 1968, the institute bears the name Centre de Logopédie and it is still the only institute of its kind in the country.

Sources

Content:

In: 1880 - 1980 Institut de Sourds-Muets. (Luxembourg), 1980.

Miesch, Liette, personal correspondence, 25 May 2004.

Steinmetz, Véronique, personal correspondence, 31 May 2013.

Illustration:

Loi du 28 janvier 1880, concernant la création d'un établissement pour l'instruction et l'éducation des sourds-muets. (La Haye), 1880:
http://www.legilux.public.lu/rgl/1880/A/0121/A.pdf

Hand alphabet:

http://legendarymedia.de/buecher/fingeralphabete-basic/luxemburg?lang=de

Figure 44: Royal Decree in The Hague

MALTA

Three persons provided information on the history of deaf education in Malta:

The first source of information was provided by Marie Alexander, professor at the University of Malta. According to Alexander a department for deaf education opened in the nineteen fifties at the Msida Primary School in Msida, to the southwest of Valletta. Joe Burlo, a trained speech therapist who studied at Manchester University, was aware that, as a colony within the British Commonwealth, Malta did not have any education for the deaf. He then received a request from the British government to find an adequate solution for this challenge. Joe Burlo temporarily went to Birmingham to learn how to educate deaf children.

Figure 45: Joe Burlo

The second source of information was Elena Tanti, who was related to Joe Burlo by marriage. Tanti said Burlo worked in Ireland as a speech therapist. In 1955, he started with education for the deaf in Malta.

The third person was Carmen Cascun, head of the Helen Keller School in Malta. Cascun stated that in 1951 the Ministry of Education of the British Commonwealth (Malta became an independent country in 1964) decided to introduce deaf education in Malta. The Ministry sent Joe Burlo back to Manchester to learn the ropes of teaching deaf children in Malta. After Burlo had returned to Malta, he was appointed as an official with the Ministry of Education of the Maltese government.

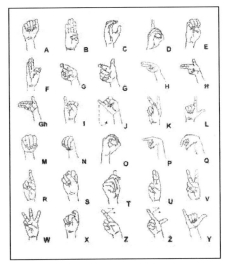

Figure 46: Maltese Hand Alphabet

The method of teaching initially used was the oral method. The pupils did however use sign language among themselves. Many years later, the method used at the school was a mix of speech and gestures. In 1956, the ministry of Education of Malta created a unit in primary education for twenty deaf pupils. In 1997 this unit was closed because it only had nine pupils. Other deaf children attended mainstream schools on Malta itself and on the country's other island Gozo. Five years later, the Skola Helen Keller was used as a school for deaf, blind and deaf-blind children. Now only four deaf children attend this school because most other deaf children attend mainstream education where they are taught by specially trained itinerant teachers.

Sources

Content:

Alexander, Marie, personal correspondence, 28 September 2005.

Cascun, Carmen, personal correspondence 7 March 2006.

Tanti, Elena, personal correspondence 6 October 2005.

Illustration:

Tanti, Elena, personal photograph

Hand alphabet:

http://www.deafmalta.com/maltese-sign-language-lsm.html (Last accessed 11 April 2013)

NETHERLANDS

Early history

As a speech therapist, Johann Conrad Ammann, originally a doctor, had a large influence on traditional deaf education in Europe, as well as on educators such as Samuel Heinicke and Charles Michel de l'Epée. The latter stated at the time that Ammann's work was one of the two torches he needed as materials in providing education. The other torch he referred to was the book by Bonet (1620).

Ammann was born in Schaffhausen (Switzerland) on 23 November 1669 and moved to Amsterdam in 1688. There he met Koolaart, a merchant, who told him that his daughter Hester was completely deaf and asked whether anything could be done about it. Ammann thus started with his speech education for a number of deaf children. Ammann's books were first published in Latin (1692) and in 1697 in Dutch and are entitled respectively: "Surdus Loquens seu methodus qua, qui surdus natus est, loqui discere possit" (Amstellaedami, 1692) and "Surdus loquens, dat is wis-konstige bijschrijvinge op wat wijse men doof-geboorene sal konnen leeren spreken".

Figure 47: Johann Conrad Ammann

All based on irrefutable grounds and supported by experience" (Haarlem, 1692). Ammann also wrote the book "Dissertatio de Loquela" in 1700 (a dissertation on speech). He died in 1724 on the country estate "Oostergeest" in Warmond.

Classroom education

On 25 November 1753, Henri Daniël Guyot was born in a parish house at Trois Fontaines, a hamlet near Liège. In 1784, Guyot, preacher of the Walloon Congregation in Groningen, arrived in Paris for a holiday. There he heard from a friend about the education of Abbé Charles Michel de l'Epée. Curious, he attended a public lesson one day. The result was that from November to late May 1785 Guyot received lessons from Abbot Charles Michel de l'Epée in Paris.

In May 1785, he began teaching in Groningen, with two pupils, one from a Reformed family and one from a Jewish family. This was quite controversial at the time but Guyot did not see it as a problem. He gave his private lessons at an upstairs room at the Brugstraat no. 3 in Groningen. He used the French method: gestures and the hand alphabet. He worked in Groningen very successfully until 1790. The public was allowed to visit his classroom once a week to see how

Guyot taught his pupils. Among others, he invited Esquire Alberda van Ekenstein and other members of the provincial council of Groningen to attend a lesson.

On 14 April 1790, Guyot and a number of businessmen founded an 'Institute to teach the Deaf and Dumb'. This signified the official start of the current Royal Dutch Kentalis and the first school for special needs education. At the time, Guyot had 14 pupils. At the inaugural meeting, a plan was made to hold a national collection to raise funds: the creation of departments in many towns and villages. The institute also received annual funding from municipal and provincial authorities and, later, from the national government. In 1808, the institute was able to acquire several buildings in the Beplante Ossenmarkt (since 1890 named after H.D. Guyot: Guyotplein) and converted them into a large building needed to house the school and boarding school.

Until his death on 10 January 1828, Guyot ran the institute together with his sons Charles and Rembt Tobie. The institute acquired worldwide renown, as is apparent from a passage in Neuman's book (1827): "…eine blühendsten und an Umfang die grösste der auf dem Continent von Europa bestehenden Anstalten dieser Art". The Parisian daily "Le Constitutionel" (1828) devoted a column to the merits of the Dutch pupil of Abbot De l'Epée:

> "Il est douteux qu'aucun Instituteur ait obtenu dans l'enseignement des sourds-muets des succès plus flatteurs, et nous ne croyons pas qu'aucun établissement du continent réunisse un plus grand nombre d'élèves, ni soit mieux tenu, sous tous les rapports que celui de Groningue." (in English: "It is doubtful whether there is anyone among the founders of schools for the deaf who has been more successful (than Guyot) and we do not think that any other institute has as many pupils or is so well maintained as the one in Groningen."

This institute had 148 pupils at the time. In 1985, the institute moved to Haren for practical reasons, where it still is today. The boarding school is housed in several smaller buildings with a small number of pupils in the south of Groningen.

Figure 48: School for the Deaf in Groningen

Today there are two organizations in the Netherlands: the Royal Auris Group in Rotterdam and Royal Dutch Kentalis with the headquarters in Sint-Michielsgestel. These organizations provide education from different locations to deaf children and youngsters. In connection with changes in education legislation and developments in the target group (neonatal hearing screening and cochlear implantation), education for the deaf in the Netherlands is in a constant state of flux.

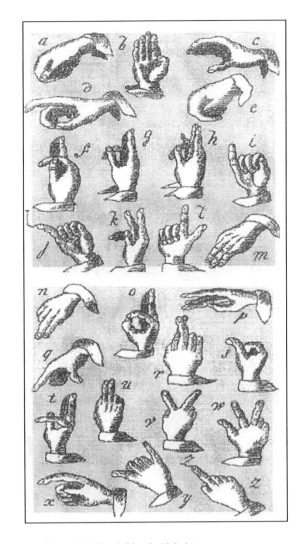

Figure 49: Dutch Hand Alphabet

Sources

Content:

Betten, H., Bevrijdend Gebaar, biography of H.D. Guyot. Library numbers 7830 and 7831 Royal Dutch Kentalis. (Groningen) 1984 and (Franeker)1990.

Büchli, M.J.C., De zorg voor de doofstomme. Library number 7868 Royal Dutch Kentalis. (Amsterdam), 1948.

Meer, J.K.H. van der, Patriotten in Groningen 1780 – 1795. Library number 7415 Royal Dutch Kentalis. (Groningen), 1996.

Neumann, F., Die Taubstummen-Anstalt zu Paris im Jahre 1822, 91. Library number 1505 Royal Dutch Kentalis. (Königsberg), 1827.

Branden, F. Jos, and Frederiks, J.G. Biografische Woordenboek der Noord- en Zuidnederlandsche letterkunde. (1888-1891).

Illustration:

School for the Deaf: Ownership of family Henk Betten.

Portrait Johann Conrad Ammann: http://www.stadtarchiv-schaffhausen.ch/Biographien/Biographien-
   HV/Ammann_Johann_Conrad,_Dr._med.,_Taubstummlehrer.pdf

Hand alphabet:

In: drawing by Johannes Lubbertus Mörser, pupil of H.D. Guyot. Library number 3142 Royal Dutch Kentalis. (Groningen),1790.

NORTHERN IRELAND

In 1826, William McComb, a teacher in mainstream education, bookseller and publisher, happened to meet William Loudon, a deaf boy, whose mother was a widow. The teacher took him on in his Brown Street School in Belfast and tried to teach him. After several years, the deaf boy showed signs of talent in drawing and painting. Sadly, several years later, William Loudon encountered an accident with fatal consequences in Glasgow.

Figure 50: Ulster Institution for the Deaf, Dumb and Blind, Lisburn Road, Belfast

Later, Claremont, the institute for the deaf, sent a number of people to Belfast on a visit. They wanted to find out if it would be possible to set up a school for the deaf in Belfast. One of the people they met was William McComb. Since the institute for the deaf in Dublin was too far for the pupils from Northern Ireland to attend, Samuel Gordon, headmaster of this institute in Dublin, sent his brother George Gordon, who was 17 years old, to Belfast to teach.

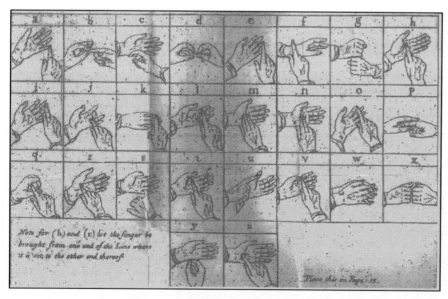

Figure 51: Northern Ireland Hand Alphabet

In 1831, the *Belfast Day School for the Deaf and Dumb* opened with seven pupils. The method used was the manual method, which Gordon brought along with him from Dublin. In those days, the classroom was located in a room at St. Anne's Cathedral on Donegal Street. One year later, a public lesson was given in order to recruit donors. In 1834, the school moved to King Street to a house in which the pupils were accommodated. A room for teaching was also rented. When the financial problems increased, a public meeting was convened on 26 March 1835. It was decided not only to focus on deaf pupils but on the education of blind children as well. This led to an increase in the number of pupils and consequently also in the financial resources. In 1845 it moved to the Lisburn Road, a site now occupied by the medical department of Queen's University. In 1961 it again moved to its present site in Jordanstown, close to the University of Ulster.

Sources

Content:

Jordanstown Journal1972 / 3. In: http://peterleach.info/jtown/history.shtml (Last accessed on 5 April 2013): In: http://en.wikipedia.org/wiki/Jordanstown_Schools

Quarterly Review of Deaf-Mute Education, 262 – 266. Volume II 1889-1890 -1891. (London), 1892.

Illustration:

Ulster Institution for the Deaf, Dumb and Blind, courtesy of the Linen Hall Library, Belfast. Source received from Mrs. Rachel Pollard, Dublin. (Belfast), no date.

Hand alphabet:

In: Digiti Lingua by Anonymus (London), 1698.

NORWAY

On 18 February 1796, Andreas Christian Møller was born in Trondheim. He was from a family of teachers and shoemakers. His father, Johannes Møller, was a shoemaker by trade and his mother's name was Ingeborg Christiansdatter Steen. When Andreas was two years old, he became deaf. In 1810, when Andreas was fourteen, his father decided to talk to Peter Olivarius Bugge, bishop of Trondheim, about his son. The bishop acted immediately and wrote a letter in Danish to the Norwegian Embassy in Copenhagen (Norwegian did not become the official language until 1850, after Norway gained independence from Denmark in 1814 after centuries of Danish rule). The letter was successful.

Figure 52: Andreas Christian Møller

In 1810, Andreas arrived in Copenhagen to register as a pupil at the school for the deaf. At school, Andreas was introduced to sign language and he learnt how to write. He stayed at the school until 1815. In 1817, Andreas Møller returned to Copenhagen to assist Dr. Peter Atke Castberg. Castberg encouraged deaf people to take up a position as a teacher at a school for the deaf, after the French example, such as Massieu. In 1822, the year when Møller returned to Trondheim, he wrote a letter to the Norwegian-Swedish king to ask for permission to teach deaf people in his native city. To his great delight, this request was granted thanks to the mediation of his old friend, the bishop of Trondheim. Castberg (1806) wrote the following words by Møller: "Some people cannot hear, they are deaf. I cannot hear. I am deaf. Years ago I was deaf and mute. Now… I am not deaf and mute, but deaf!"

An article by Odd-Inge Schröder tells us that Møller, 21 years old, taught four adult deaf people by means of sign language for ten years. The school for the deaf in Trondheim was founded by Royal Decree on 1 November 1824 but it took until 1 April of the following year before the actual teaching began. Møller started with seven pupils and by the end of the year there were 20. The list of income and expenses shows that Andreas Møller and Peter, his seven year younger brother, received their salary once per quarter. But with the following difference: Andreas earned twice as much as his brother. Their father was in charge of the boarding school for boys and girls, while Johan Julius Dircks and Pehr Pehrson, a Swedish national, who were both deaf, also worked there as teachers. As a headmaster and teacher Andreas met with much appreciation in Trondheim and the surrounding areas. In addition, the government in Oslo (formerly Kristiania) helped them as much as possible, both morally and financially, although the government would rather have seen Oslo as the main city for the national education for the deaf.

On 26 April 1826, Andreas married Birgitte Marie Holst, the daughter of a clergyman, who was born on 4 August 1804. They had nine children, including twins. According to the 1875 article from the Throndhjems Døvstumme-Institut Andreas quit his job as a headmaster in 1845.

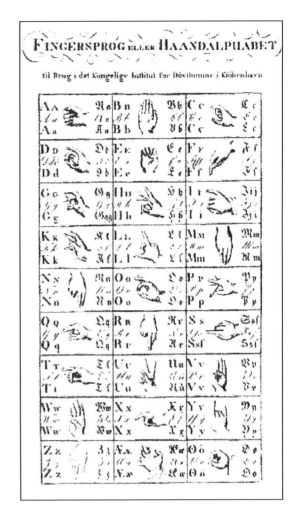

Figure 53: Norwegian Hand Alphabet

Sources

Content:

Castberg, P.A., Første Lesebog for Døvstumme. Library number 1150 Royal Dutch Kentalis. (København), 1806.

Schroder, Odd-Inge, Introduction to the History of Norwegian Sign Language. In: Looking Back a reader on the history of languages, by Renate Fischer and Harlan Lane (eds.), 232–233. Library number 6106 Royal Dutch Kentalis. (Hamburg), 1993.

Shavlan, Sigvald, Throndhjems Døvstumme-Institut. (Throndjhem), 1875 / 1876.

Skjølberg, Trygve, Andreas Christian Møller 1796–1874. (Bergen), 1989.

Sander, Anne-Kirstin, personal correspondence, 25 August 1992.

Skjølberg, Trygve, personal correspondence, 20 September 1988.

Illustration:

Fotografering: 1850 - 1860 (CA) Produsent, sikker: Peder O.Aune. Sverresborg Trøndelag Folkemuseum. (Trondheim), 1860.

Hand alphabet:

"Forelaesninger over Dövstumme Undervisningens Methode, holdne i Pastoralseminariet i Kjöbenhavn. Med Kobber over et Haandalfabet." Library number 1152 Royal Dutch Kentalis. (København), 1818.

POLAND

Figure 54: Institute of the Deaf, Dumb and Blind in Warsaw

On 23 October 1817, Jakub Falkowski, a clergyman, founded a school for the deaf at Warsaw. He was also the first Polish teacher of the deaf. He was born on 29 April 1775 in Budlewo near Siemiatycze.

In 1802, he took charge of a seven year old deaf boy and tried to teach him how to speak, but he was not very successful. After a year, Falkowski went to Berlin to familiarize himself with the teaching method at a school for the deaf there. He learnt the German method: speaking and mimicking. This presented Falkowski with a second chance. Back in Warsaw, he started to teach a young deaf boy at a school for hearing children. After two years, Falkowski felt confident enough to introduce his pupil to the Commission for Education and Science. They gave the go ahead for the foundation of an institute for the deaf in Warsaw and the job was open for anyone who wanted to give it a try. However, for many years no one took up the challenge.

Jakub Falkowski himself had meanwhile left for Vienna to register as a student in order to obtain the certificate of teacher of the deaf. Eventually, thanks to his efforts, the first school for the deaf in Poland opened on 23 October 1817. Despite a lack of accommodation and very limited financial resources for the new institute the founder and teacher persevered with his life's work.

After ten years of fruitless requests for better housing, donations and other support, the institute was finally able to move to the location where it still can be found today. The education for the deaf in Warsaw was based on the oral method; the pupils were taught to speak and mimic mouth movements.

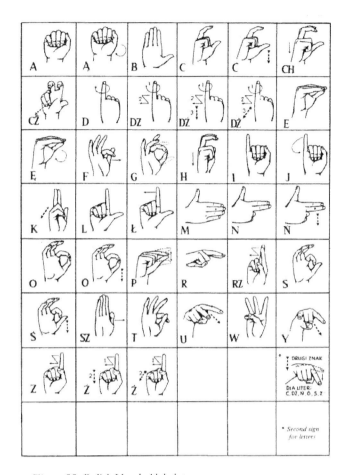

Figure 55: Polish Hand Alphabet

Sources

Content:

Lipkowski, Otton, 150 years of schools for the Deaf in Poland. (Warsaw), 1967.

170 LAT Instytutu Gluchoniemych im. Jakuba Falkowskiego W. Warszawie 1817 – 1987. (Warsaw), 1987

Personal correspondence, 3 July 1990 by Instytut Gluchoniemych, Warszawa.

Illustration:

Lipkowski, O., 150 years of schools for the deaf in Poland. Library number 3678-a, Royal Dutch Kentalis. (Warsaw) 1967.

Hand alphabet:

In: International Hand Alphabet Charts, second edition, edited and compiled by Simon J. Carmel. (Rockville, Md, USA), 1982

PORTUGAL

Early history

The first Portuguese speech therapist who worked in French deaf education was Jacobo Rodríguez Pereira. Rodríguez Pereira was born on 11 April 1715 at Berlanga. Between 1734 and 1780, in Paris, he taught a total of twelve pupils how to speak and he also used a hand alphabet, which was, however, based on phonetic properties. Pupils were allowed to mimic gestures but no more than that. As with the German teacher Samuel Heinicke, Pereira's teaching method was surrounded by secrecy.

Classroom teaching

The 'Jacobo Rodríguez Pereira' school for the deaf was officially opened in Lisbon on 20 April 1823 thanks to the efforts of crown princess Maria, who persuaded João VI of Portugal, her hard of hearing father (according to Hüls, Rainier), to found this school. So far, the school did not yet have any teaching staff. The king therefore searched all over Europe and finally found Pär Aron Borg, the founder and director of the institute for the deaf in Stockholm, willing to run the new school. The school found accommodation in the building "Conde de Mesquitela". The Swede introduced the manual method after the example of Abbé De l'Epée, and taught 12 pupils, who were all boarders. He only stayed there for four years. The reason was that his life was in danger. In 1828, Lisbon was ruled by Don Miguel with a reign of terror. On page 69 of "De Gids" (1864) it is written:

Figure 56: Pär Aron Borg

> "….however, when the pig and man slaughterer Don Miguel ruled there, Borg, so as not to be murdered as a Freemason, had to leave his institution and returned to Sweden."

He never returned to finish his work for the Portuguese school. Until this day, they use the Swedish hand alphabet. Ten years later, on 15 February 1834, the school was integrated by Royal Decree with the Casa Pia in Lisbon.

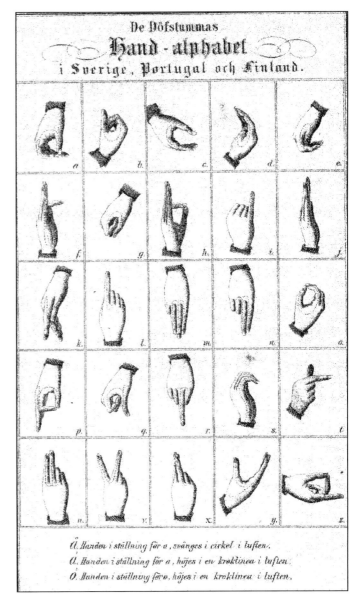

Figure 57: Portuguese Hand Alphabet

Sources

Content:

Hüls, Rainier, Die Geschichte der Hörakustik, 77-78. Library number 7182 Royal Dutch Kentalis. (Heidelberg), 1999.

"De Gids" 1864, 28e jaargang, Het doofstommenonderwijs 3e serie.

Antunes, Manuel Lobo, personal correspondence, 9 November 1988.

Illustration:

In: Bilderatlas zur Geschichte der Taubstummenbildung by Ernst Emmerig. Library number 5530 Royal Dutch Kentalis. (München), 1927.

Hand alphabet:

Borg, E., Om Institutet för dövstumma och blinda. 1. (Stockholm), 1854.

ROMANIA

Figure 58: Princess Elena Cuza

The oldest Romanian school for the deaf can be found in the small town of Dumbraveni near Brasov, which was founded by the Romanian national Ioan C. Bacila, a hussar from Napoleon's army. He is said to have had an opportunity to visit the institute for the blind and deaf in Paris. The method he used was therefore the French model: gestures and finger spelling. The school ran from 1831 to 1846. Unfortunately, no further information is available about this school.

The first institute for the deaf set up by the State, was the department for the deaf which was part of the Princess Elena institute in Bucharest. The initiative for this was taken by Dr. Carol Davila (1828-1884), managing director for health matters, who in 1860 organized a project for the formation of a Commission of social welfare for orphans and children with special needs.

This project received the backing of Princess Elena Cuza, the wife of Alexandru Ioan Cuza, the reigning sovereign, and in 1862 the construction of the Princess Elena building commenced. For years, the institute received financial support from Princess Elena. Another important contribution to this project was made by Vasile Alecsandri, the greatest poet and dramatist of his age, and one of the greatest Romanian authors of all time. He donated his latest manuscript with poems to the project, including all the financial rights that rested on it.

The first deaf children arrived at the special section of the institute on 15 November 1863. Although only few documents about the education methods remain, it is assumed that the oral method was used. The methods were derived from the French school and the school itself employed a French teacher, who was deaf himself.

In 1895, the department for the education of the deaf moved to the town of Focsani, where it became a school for children with special needs and where it is still located today.

Two personalities left their mark on the special needs education of those days:

1. Ion Cioranescu (1874-1948). He was the author of the first-year handbook for deaf children, published in 1932 in Cernauti. As an adherent of the oral method, he adopted methods from German deaf education. He was the first who made a division into classes for his deaf pupils, the criterion being the level of their linguistic development, and not their intelligence or extent of deafness.

2. Dimitrie Rusticeanu, (1884-1942) writer of many textbooks for mainstream and special education. In Vienna, he attended lessons in education for the blind and later education for the deaf. Although he was interested in the oral method, and was also an advocate of this method, he was very receptive to sign language as well. He introduced it as a means to teach speech and wrote an original work, the first in Romania, about this subject. He also compiled a dictionary/glossary with illustrations for deaf children. The manuscript of this book has been preserved.

There is also a special infant school and a school for primary and secondary education for the Hungarian minority. These schools can be found all over the country. They are mainly boarding schools and are therefore located near to the children's home towns. Nowadays, deaf children are increasingly being integrated into mainstream schools.

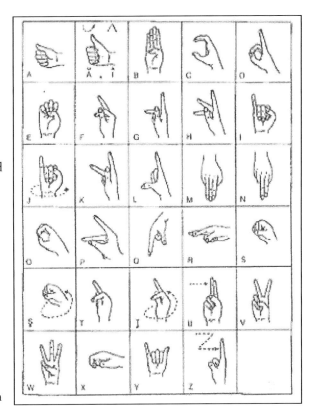

Figure 59: Romanian Hand Alphabet

Sources

Content:
Dumitrana, Magdalena, personal correspondence, 7 July 1995.

Illustration:
Found on 29 July 2009. In: commons.wikimedia.org/wiki/File:Elena_Cuza.jpeg. Scanned from an issue of Magazin Istoric, 1860s. Author: unknown.

Hand alphabet:
In: International Hand Alphabet Charts, second edition, edited and compiled by Simon J. Carmel. (Rockville, Md, USA), 1982.

RUSSIA

The first Russian school for deaf children was founded in 1806 by Czarina Maria Feodorovna, daughter-in-law of Catharine the Great and mother-in-law of King William II of the Netherlands. The reason for its foundation is remarkable: Alexander Meller, one of the first pupils, wrote an autobiography in 1872 in which this story is related[6]. The son of a Major General, he heard from his aunt how in the summer of 1806 he was walking with her in the park in the palace grounds of Czar Paul I and Czarina Maria Feodorovna. By chance, they met Maria Feodorovna, who was told that Alexander was deaf. She gently touched the boy's cheek and showered him with sweets. The next day, they met again and the widow spoke the following words to Alexander's aunt:

> "Last night, I could not sleep because Alexander's deafness kept me awake. I will go to Williamov, my secretary and have him find out if it is possible to set up a school for the deaf soon".

Figure 60: Czarina Maria Feodorovna with Alexander Meller

The aunt broke into tears of gratitude and she kissed the Czarina's hand to thank her.

Father Anselm Sigmund, who had visited the Viennese school for the deaf, arrived from Poland not long after that to set up a new school for the deaf in the fortress of Marienthal in Pavlovsk. He started in 1806 with four boys and five girls.

Every afternoon, the Czarina personally visited Pavlovsk to bring milk, butter and other food for the pupils. She also spent 4500 rubles of her own money on two things: 2660 roubles for the salaries of teachers and their assistants and 1840 rubles for clothing and food for the pupils. In 1808, the Czarina no longer liked Father Sigmund's way of teaching and she wrote in a letter to Sicard that, although Sigmund was an excellent teacher, he failed in his duty to instruct the pupils in religious

---

[6] The first document of Alexander Meller is a letter, dated 1872, written to P.I. Stepanov, at that time Director at the St. Petersburg Institute, in reply to an inquiry that Stepanov had send him on 15 February of that year. This letter (reproduced in Lagovsy 1910, pp. 9-13) shows details of a chance meeting between himself and the tsarina Maria Feodorovna in the gardens of Pavlovsk Palace near St. Petersburg in the summer of 1806, which prompted her to set up and endow a school for Meller and other Deaf children.

matters. She also demanded that the new French teacher spoke excellent Russian. In reply, the institute for the deaf in Paris recommended Jean-Baptiste Jauffret as Sigmund's successor and, his qualities being excellent, he was engaged. Sicard also suggested to have Laurent Clerc join him but Maria Feodorovna refused because the budget only allowed for one person to qualify for a travel allowance. Father Sigmund returned to his home country, much to the distress of his pupils.

After the number of pupils had risen spectacularly, in 1810 the Czarina had the school moved to a large building on the Gorokhovaya in St. Petersburg. This building remained a school for the deaf until 1965.

In 1995, the center of deaf education returned to its former location Pavlovsk. In 1995, an art academy was also opened for 150 deaf and several hard of hearing students from all over Russia. Students are trained as professional artists and specialists to teach at schools for the deaf. The course lasts five years.

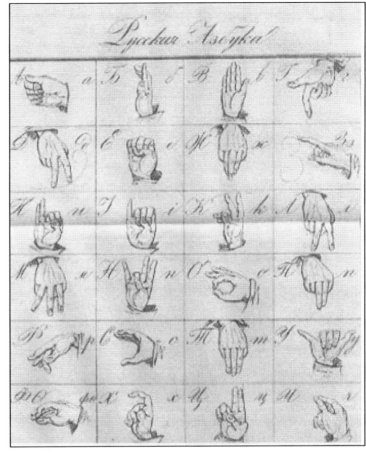

Figure 61: Russian Hand Alphabet

Sources:

Content:

Emmerig, Ernst, Bilderatlas zur Geschichte der Taubstummenbildung. Library number 5530 Royal Dutch Kentalis (München), 1927.

Lagovsky, N.M., S.-Peterburgskoe Uchilishche Glukhhonemykh (1810-1910), (St. Petersburg), 1910.

Williams, Harold G. and Fyodorova, Polina, The origins of the St.Petersburg Institute for the Deaf, In: Looking Back, a reader on the history of languages, by Renate Fischer en Harlan Lane (eds.). Library number 6106 Royal Dutch Kentalis (Hamburg), 1995, 295-305.

Williams, Harold G. Deaf teachers in 19th Century Russia. In: Looking Back, a reader on the history of languages, by Renate Fischer and Harlan Lane (eds.) 109. Library number 6106 Royal Dutch Kentalis (Hamburg), 1995.

Ons Bondsblad, April / May 1997, article.

Illustration:

Picture by Mr. Gennady Fadin (deaf painter at Moscow), n.d. Source: Mr. Jan Backer, The Netherlands.

Hand alphabet:

In: Gloucho njémie, rassmatriwaembi cet by Viktor Fleury . Library number 1176 Royal Dutch Kentalis. (St. Petersburg), 1835.

SCOTLAND

Thomas Braidwood (1715 – 1806) initially worked as a teacher's assistant at a secondary school in Hamilton, while later he opened a school for mathematics in Edinburgh. In 1760, he taught a deaf pupil for the first time. Quite remarkable about the education for the deaf in Scotland is the fact that three generations of the Scottish Braidwood family encompassed three countries in 64 years: Scotland, England, and the United States.

PLATE V. School for the Deaf and Dumb, Edinburgh, 1819. From an uncopyrighted photograph in the Edinburgh Library.

PLATE VI. Donaldson's Hospital, School for Deaf and Dumb, Edinburgh, 1850. From an uncopyrighted photograph in the Edinburgh Library.

Figure 62: School for the Deaf and Dumb, Edinburgh, 1819 & 1850

Thomas Braidwood was born as the youngest child of the family of Thomas and Agnes (Meek) in a 15th century farmhouse called "Hillhead" in Covington and Thankerton in the district of Lanarkshire. He studied in Edinburgh. As an interesting aside: quite near to these places there is a village called Braidwood, which currently has a population of over 600 inhabitants.

During the first quarter of 1760, Alexander Shirreff, a wealthy merchant, took his deaf son Charles to Thomas Braidwood's school on the eastern side of St. Leonard's Road (now: Dumbiedykes Road) in Edinburgh. This academy became known by the nickname Dummie House and closed in 1873. On Kirkwood's map of Edinburgh, published in 1817, the name 'Dumbie House' can be read, which later became known as 'Craigside'. The building was demolished in 1939.

The method used by Braidwood was writing, speaking and mimicking mouth movements. To communicate, he used the two-handed finger alphabet. Raymond Lee (1997) assumes that Braidwood used the book

"Grammatica Linguae Anglicanae. Cui praefigitur, De Loquela sive Sonorum Formatione" (Oxford: Leonard Lichfield, 1653), as a basis for his teaching.

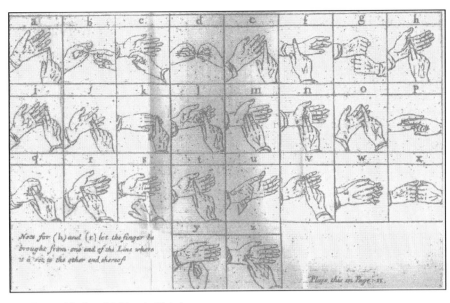

Figure 63: Scottish Hand Alphabet

It is said of Charles Shirreff (1750 – 1831), Braidwood's very first pupil that he became a highly successful miniature portrait painter in London, Bath, Brighton, and in the West Indies. Braidwood had another remarkable student: John Goodricke, born in Groningen in 1764, son of a diplomat, who had immigrated to Scotland with his parents when he was 6 years old. He became a world famous astronomer and a member of the Royal Society. Sadly, he died of pneumonia at a young age in 1786. Another highly gifted and deaf born pupil of Braidwood's was Francis Humbertstone MacKenzie, a future parliamentarian and governor of Barbados.

Raymond Lee (1997) 'complains' in his work that very little has been written about how things exactly went at the school, but the same goes for nearly all early schools for the deaf that we know of. He asks himself whether or not the children were resident pupils and whether or not they studied and slept in the same building "Dumbie House". John Braidwood, probably a cousin of Thomas, started in 1770 as an assistant in deaf education and later he also played a significant part in this profession. In his travel diary, Samuel Johnson wrote that in 1773 the school had about 20 pupils.

On page 113 of her book, Ruth Bender (1960) elaborates on the arrival of Mr. Francis Green from America in 1780 at Braidwood's school to have his deaf son Charles receive education. In America there were no schools for the deaf until 1817.

In 1783, Braidwood received a letter from King George III. The King wanted to see a school for the deaf in London and he considered Braidwood the right person to set one up. He promised him 100 guineas as a reward. Braidwood complied with this request and moved to Hackney, in those days a suburb to the east of London. He continued to work for his school almost until the day he died. In 1806 Thomas Braidwood was buried on the cemetery next to the Presbyterian Dissenters' Chapel in Hackney.

In 1810, Thomas Braidwood's grandson continued to teach deaf children in Edinburgh.

Sources

Content:

The Braidwood Family. In: American Annals of the Deaf and Dumb. Vol. XXII. (1878)

Arnold, Thomas, Aures Surdis, The Education of the Deaf and Dumb, 66. (London), 1879.

Bender, Ruth E., The conquest of deafness. Library number 3509 Royal Dutch Kentalis. (Cleveland 6, Ohio), 1960.

Hay, John and Lee, Raymond, Braidwood 1715 – 1806. In: Deaf History journal, Vol. 1 Issue 1, April 1997. (Feltham), 1997.

Jackson, Peter, Britain's Deaf Heritage. (Edinburgh), 1990.

Lee, Raymond, Braidwoodian Buildings and Locations, published by British History Deaf Society, (Feltham), 2001.

Illustration:

Uncopyrighted photograph in the Edinburgh library: in: Bender, Ruth E., The conquest of deafness, page 96. (after) (Cleveland 6, Ohio), 1960.

Hand alphabet:

In: Digiti Lingua by Anonymous. (London), 1698.

SERBIA

The school for the deaf in Sremska Mitrovica is the oldest school of its kind in Serbia, which until 1918 was part of the Austrian Empire. That was why Radivoje Popovic went to the institute for the deaf in Vienna to learn the skills needed. He started to work as a teacher of deaf children in 1886. Further details are lacking.

The second school for the deaf in Serbia was founded in Belgrade on 10 October 1893 by the Freemasons' Lodge "Dobrotvor" ("Benefactor"), but teaching did not start

Figure 64: School for the Deaf in Belgrade

until 3 January 1897. It was a private school set up by King Decanski (Kralj Dec) and the school also bears his name. The reason for the foundation of this school was to save deaf children from the inhumane conditions they lived in, such as poverty and begging.

In those days, the oral method was the official method used in education but sign language was also used as an aid, especially for children with learning difficulties.

Figure 65: Yugoslavian Hand Alphabet (1894)

The school started in 1897 with 12 pupils. From this date to 1941 a total of 500 pupils had 'graduated'. Until 1941, the school was funded by the State but in that year the Germans first closed the school and then destroyed the building. The school made a restart in 1945 in a new building and it is still there today.

In 1990, Serbia had a total of 9 schools for the deaf each with a boarding school, where pupils receive free education.

Sources

Content:

Slavica Jelic, personal correspondence.30 April 2013.

Savic, Ljubomir M., personal correspondence, 1 February 1994.

Illustration & hand alphabet:

Slavica Jelic

SLOVAKIA

Figure 66: School for the Deaf in Kremnica

On 30 May 1903, the Minister of Education of Hungary, which was part of the Austro-Hungarian Empire, inquired by letter about the possibility of founding a new school for deaf pupils in Kremnica. The council for medical educational sciences then explored the possibilities to help children with hearing problems and their families in Slovakia. In those days, these children did not go to school but wandered around. There was some minor resistance from people in Kremnica and also from some members of the municipal council. This resistance was overcome by Koloman Hercsuth thanks to his lectures together with teachers of the Institute for the deaf in Budapest about the importance and the need for such a school. Koloman Hercsuth was a friend of the mayor of Kremnica and convinced of the idea that an institute of the deaf was needed[7].

In 1906, Koloman Hercsuth started with 12 pupils in Kremnica. Under the influence of the controversial decision of the Milan Conference of 1880, the oral method of teaching was adopted. The salaries of the staff were paid for by the Hungarian government, while the school itself was managed by the municipality of Kremnica and environs. After 1914, the institute received its own building.

In 1919, Czechoslovakia seceded from Austria and Hungary and the responsibility for the institute now rested with the Ministry of Education of Czechoslovakia. After an agreement had been signed between the ministries of Education and Trade, the latter decided in 1922 to raise the level of the institute by adding new departments: a technical school, shoemaking and (ladies) outfitting.

Since 1957, the method used by pupils at the institutes in Kremnica, Bratislava and Prešov is the originally Spanish hand alphabet as described in the book by Bonet (1620).

---

[7] http://zsispkremnica.edupage.org/text2/ (last accessed 14 May 2013)

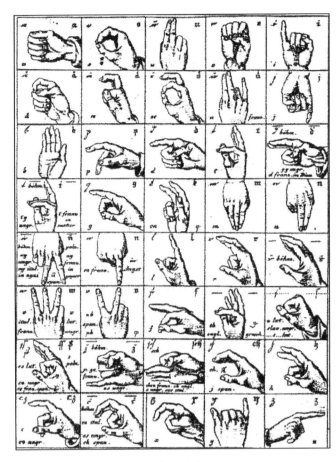

Figure 67: Slovakian Hand Alphabet

Sources

Content:

Licko, Jozef, personal correspondence, 15 March 2006.

Illustration:

Licko, Jozef

Hand alphabet:

Czech, F.H., Versinnlichte Denk- und Sprachlehrere, mit Anwendung auf die Religions- und Sittenlehre und auf das Leben. Library number 24 Royal Dutch Kentalis.(Wien), 1836.

SLOVENIA

Valentin Stanic, who was born in 1774 in Bodrez and died in 1847 in Gorica, was an Austrian priest, researcher, and teacher. Stanic once came across a book by Franz Herman Czech, an Austrian, about education for the deaf. He later met several deaf people, who had previously been taught by two teachers.

Figure 68: Valentin Stanic

As a priest, Stanic founded a school in Gorica on 22 April 1840. It is the oldest school of its kind in the former Yugoslavia. Stanic started teaching when he had raised sufficient funds. He had eleven pupils, seven of which were boys.

Stanic ignored the advice of Czech, a strong advocate of the oral method, and decided to use the manual method. In 1884, under the influence of the Milan Conference, it was decided to adopt oralism after all. Because the financial situation had meanwhile improved, the private school was converted into an institute for the deaf. Later, Stanic received financial support from the Austro-Hungarian Empire.

Slovenia currently has three schools for the deaf. The largest is in the capital, Ljubljana. Other schools can be found in Portoroz and Maribor. The latter school stills uses the oral method.

Sources

Content:

Ziva Peljhan, personal correspondence September 2003.

Grosses Kongressbuch ueber den III. Weltkongress der Gehörlosen in Wiesbaden, 325–326.Library number 3754 Royal Dutch Kentalis. (Frankfurt am Main) 1959.

Illustration:

Found on October 2006:http://sl.wikipedia.org/wiki/Valentin_Stani%C4%8D

Hand alphabet:

Ziva Peljhan.

Figure 69: Slovenian Hand Alphabet

SPAIN

Early history

Ponce de Léon, a Benedict monk of noble descent, is said to have given private lessons around 1545 to ten or twelve deaf students from families of noblemen and high ranking officials in the monastery of San Salvador de Ofia near Burgos. This monk did not leave any textbook on his teaching methods. Written and oral evidence show that he initially taught his pupils by means of writing, whereby a direct connection was made between object and symbol. How Ponce taught speech the documents do not tell us but it is certain that his pupils were able to speak to some degree. There is no mention of mimicking and communication was through writing or the hand alphabet. Some of the pupils appear to have reached a good level of development.

Manuel Ramirez de Carrion (1579 –1652) was a schoolteacher by trade and gained a reputation by introducing a phonetic reading method instead of the usual alphabetical method and which helped him teach his pupils how to read in just a couple of weeks. His first deaf pupil was the future Marquis Don Alonso Fernandez de Priego, nicknamed "El Mudo". Thanks to the written instruction he received, he developed so well that "El Mudo" was widely regarded as a wise Christian sovereign.

Juan Martin Pablo Bonet (1579 – 1633) wrote the very first textbook for deaf education in the world, which was greatly influenced by De Carrion. The beautifully illustrations of the alphabet drawn by Yebra can still be admired in this book, which was published in 1620.

Classroom teaching

Esther de los Santos stated in a personal email correspondence that it is not easy to pinpoint when after 1760 classroom teaching actually began. The information available is of a rather general and confusing nature.

The first private school, which was called "Colego Nacional de Sordomudos", opened in 1775 and was converted into an institute for the deaf on 9 January 1805. The opening was performed by King Carlos IV, encouraged by Manuel de Godoy, an important politician. They attended for humanitarian reasons knowing that their presence would ensure publicity for the institute. Unfortunately, there is no mention of the identities of the first teachers. But several names have been passed down: José Miguell

Figure 70: Ponce de Léon

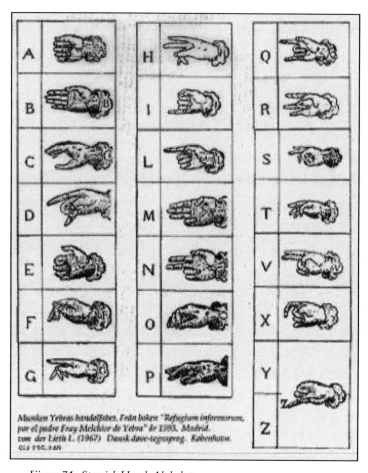

Figure 71: Spanish Hand Alphabet

Alea and Roberto Francisco Prádez, who meant a great deal for deaf education in its early years. The responsibility for deaf education now rested with the economic committee of the city of Madrid.

The method used before the Milan Conference was a mixture of the oral and the manual methods. Unfortunately, no further information is available. We do not know, therefore, with how many pupils this education started.

Sources

Content:

Büchli, M.J.C., De zorg voor de doofstomme, 20 - 25. Library number 7868 Royal Dutch Kentalis. (Amsterdam), 1948.

Santos, Esther de los, personal correspondence, November, 16th, 1990, with list of literature.

http://en.wikipedia.org/wiki/Pedro_Ponce_de_León (last accessed on 20 May 2013)

Illustration:

In: magazine: Revista de la enseñanza de los sordomudos y de los ciegos. Library T. number 2, Royal Dutch Kentalis. (Madrid), 1851.

Hand alphabet:

Libro Llamado Refugium Infirmorum by Melchor de Yebra. (Madrid), 1593.

SWEDEN

Early history

The first teacher of the deaf in Sweden and Finland was Abraham Argillander. He was born in 1722 as the son of a Lutheran preacher in Kuopio in the Duchy of Finland, which was then still part of the Swedish Kingdom. In 1756, he married Maria Helsingius, who had a deaf brother.

In 1762, Argillander was asked to teach deaf sisters. He used manual gestures. An article was devoted to this in "The Proceedings of the Royal Swedish Academy of Sciences in 1771" (Jossfolk, 2001). It describes in detail Argillander's method of teaching. He let his pupils make gestures and taught them how to write. Step by step, he taught them how to pronounce the Swedish alphabet. He continued to do so until they finally understood it. Argillander also taught his deaf brother-in-law Wolfgang Henrik how to read and write. Unfortunately, Argillander gave up teaching.

Classroom teaching

On 6 June 1809, thanks to the efforts of Pär Aron Borg (1776 – 1839), an institute for the deaf opened its doors in Stockholm. Borg was a civil servant at the Chancellery. The school was first located in a rented building at the Regeringsgatan but later moved to the Drottninggatan. In 1812, Borg managed to acquire this picturesque but neglected building for his school in the district of Djurgården. The institute had the good fortune of receiving a gift from Mr. Corral, the Spanish ambassador, who donated a piece of his land. It was a time of hard work because a new classroom, bedrooms, and a dining room needed to be built.

Pär Aron Borg first started teaching blind pupils. Once, he visited a theatrical performance of a piece by Bouilly about the deaf son of a count. This sparked his interest in education for the deaf. He was a manager and

Figure 72: School for the Deaf in Stockholm

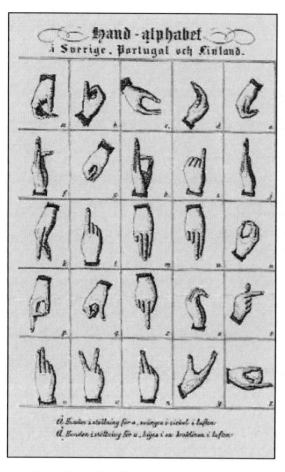

Figure 73: Swedish Hand Alphabet

therefore did not teach himself. He left this to others. Borg also taught his pupils to do manual work: dressmaking, shoemaking, carpentry, painting, etc. For the girls this meant spinning, weaving, sewing, etc. The institute attracted the interest of the Royal Family. Borg once gave a demonstration lesson for no less than 500 people including the Royal Family. The government subsequently gave an annual subsidy for deaf education.

The teaching method used was the manual method. Borg invented his own hand alphabet, which, with one or two changes in the hand positions, is still used in Sweden, Finland and Portugal to this day. At the time of Borg's death, the institute had 50 pupils but only two teachers.

Sources

Content:

Åser, Hammar, article: The Manilla School for the Deaf (Stockholm), n.d. Londen, Monica, Communicational choices for Minorities within Minorities, the case of the Finland – Swedish Deaf. University Helsinki. Departement of Education Research. Report 193. (Helsinki), 2004.

Sayers, William, A Treatise from Enlightenment Sweden on Teaching the Mute to Read and Speak. In: Journal of Deaf Studies and Deaf Education, Fall 1999.

Lavold, Anne-Berit, personal correspondence, 16 February 2004.

Illustration:

Manilla Dövstumskola 1812 – 1912 by Johan Prawitz, 205. Library number 8090 Royal Dutch Kentalis. (Stockholm), 1913.

Hand alphabet:

Borg, E., Om Institutet för dëstumma och blinda. 1 (Stockholm). Library number 1736 Royal Dutch Kentalis. (Stockholm), 1854.

SWITZERLAND

Early history

From 1646, the Swiss Johannes Lavater (1624 - 1695) studied for a while at the University of Groningen. One of his teachers there was Anthonius Deusing, who had a large influence on Lavater about the possibilities of deaf education. Büchli (1948) states that Lavater wrote about a method for deaf education, which contained a recommendation for writing and the hand alphabet. It was then proposed to set up a school for the deaf and a collection was subsequently held among the rich of the city of Zürich. But no school for the deaf was founded. In 1664, in a dissertation Lavater also wrote about the causes of deafness. He wondered whether the damage to a nerve branch could lead to the loss of speech.

Classroom teaching

In 1777, the priest and physician Heinrich Keller (1728 - 1802) ran a private school for deaf children at Schlieren near Zürich, the first in Switzerland. The 49-year old teacher got the idea to teach deaf children after he had read the book by Johann Conrad Ammann. In 1779, Keller appointed Johann Conrad Ulrich as a new teacher. Three years later, Ulrich went to Paris to attend the lessons of Abbé De l'Epée. When he had learnt enough, he returned to Zürich to found a school for the deaf. To his disappointment, nothing came of it. Why this was so, remains unclear.

When Johann Conrad Ulrich (1761 – 1828) was staying in Paris, Abbé De l'Epée gave him his letters which were intended for Heinrich Keller and the academic gymnasium in Zurich. The teachers there were to study the correspondence between De l'Epée and Heinicke to decide which method was most suitable for deaf education: the manual method or the oral method. Keller was also asked to give his advice. Keller was obviously aware of the contents of this correspondence and after he had read a report by Ulrich he chose a mixed method for his own teaching. The method comprised:

Figure 74: School for the Deaf in Yverdon

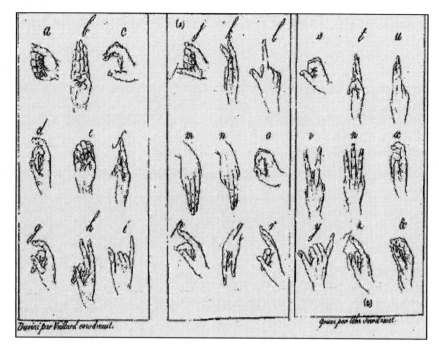

Figure 75: Swiss Hand Alphabet

manual gestures and use of the hand alphabet, teaching the spoken language, lip-reading, and writing.

Keller taught until about 1793, while his household was run by his sister. Thanks to his membership of the "Moralischen Gesellschaft", Keller received financial support for his work as a teacher. One of the aims of this society was to help poor and disabled people. Keller also wrote a new textbook, entitled *Versuch über die beste Lehrart, Taubstumme zu unterrichten*, which was published in 1786.

On 1 July 1811, the first official institute for the deaf in Switzerland was founded at Yverdon by Johann Konrad Naef (1789 – 1843), a pupil of Ulrich. He was supported by Pestalozzi, the famous educator, who had founded a school for the poor there in 1807. The method used by Naef for his education was the same as Keller's. He started with ten boys. During the first two years after its foundation, Naef had to pay for the school himself but later he received subsidy from the State. Unfortunately, this was not sufficient and he had to look for other resources, which he found in charities. After a while, he was succeeded as the institute's director by Karl Naef, his son, who worked as a chemist. In 1868, the institute moved to Moudon.

Sources

Content:

Beglinger, Heinrich, personal correspondence, 21 February 1993.

Büchli, M.J.C., De zorg voor de doofstomme. Library number 7868 Royal Dutch Kentalis. (Amsterdam), 1948.

Caramore, Benno, Die Gebärdensprache in der Schweizerischen Gehörlosenpädagogik des 19, Jahrhunderts. (Hamburg), 1988.

Emmerig, Ernst, Bilderatlas zur Geschichte der Taubstummenbildung. Library number 5530 Royal Dutch Kentalis. (München), 1927.

Keller, Heinrich, Versuch über die beste Lehrart, Taubstumme zu unterrichten. (Zurich), 1786.

Werner, Hans, Johannes Lavaters Taubstummenschule. In: Blätter für Taubstummenbildung, 40. Jahrg. nr. 19, October, 1, 1927.

Illustration:

Sutermeister, Eugen (deaf), Quellenbuch zur Geschichte des Schweizerischen Taubstummenwesens. Page 253. Band 1 en 2. Library number 3374 Royal Dutch Kentalis. (Bern), 1929.

Hand alphabet :

In: L'Alphabet Manuel by Isaäc, Etienne Chomel. (deaf founder and educator of the Institute for the deaf child in Geneva) Library number 420 Royal Dutch Kentalis (Geneva), 1800.

TURKEY[8]

The author Ludger Busse wrote in a number of articles that the sources of education for blind and deaf people in Turkey were very limited. He gratefully availed himself of the article "Sagirlar ve Dilsizler" by Ali Haydar, published in 1925 in a Turkish magazine called 'Muamlimler Mecmuasi'.

In 1924, Haydar visited a school for the deaf, which gives us some idea of when education for blind and deaf pupils started during the Ottoman period.

Figure 76: School for the Deaf in Istanbul

In 1883, Ferdi Garati, an Austrian, addressed a petition to the Ottoman government with the request to open a commercial school in Istanbul. Encouraged by the good results and the contacts he had made, he submitted another petition to the government in 1889, this time with the request to open a school for deaf pupils. Late September that same year, he was allowed to start his school in a building where the commercial school was also housed. Garati took on pupils, irrespective of their nationality and religion. The government paid for the education. But there was still no facility for resident pupils. The subjects taught included language, reading and writing, speech, religion, arithmetic, geography, and physical education. When it first opened, the school had 25 to 30 pupils and the year after this number grew to 45.

The school was managed by Besim Bey, son of the then well-known educationalist Selim Sabit. Another man, Hüseyin Sabri Bey, was appointed as a teacher and also as supervisory official for the building of the commercial school. They used sign language and the hand alphabet as a method of communication for their teaching. When the pupils were 6 to

---

[8] During the Deaf History International Conference in Paris in July 2003, Patricia Raswant from the USA delivered a lecture entitled "Istanbul's Topkapi: Ixarette, the language of Mutes in the 15th, 16th and 17th centuries". She presented how deaf people and dwarfs from the conquered regions of Europe were taken to Istanbul by the Ottoman army by order of the sultan. At court, they were only allowed to use sign language to communicate (the word ixarette means sign language in Turkish). The little information that is available in Turkey about this history was taken from reports of travelers from the West who visited the Ottoman Empire between the 16th and 18th centuries.

8 years old, they could be admitted to this education. One year later, the school also received a department for blind pupils. Before the education for the deaf stopped in 1926, the school had 16 pupils including only one girl, divided among three classrooms. Why the education stopped in 1926 is not clear from the sources. Perhaps the changed political situation in the country had something to do with it. The year 1923 was the end of the Ottoman Empire. Mustafa Kemal Atatürk seized power and became the first president of Turkey.

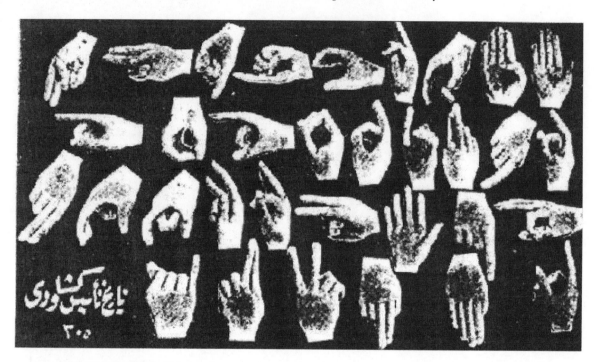

Figure 77: Ottoman Hand Alphabet

Sources

Content:
Busse, Ludger, Ferdi Garati und seine Schule für Gehörlose und Blinde in Istanbul – Die Ursprünge des türkischen Sonderschulwesens. In magazine: Hörpad, 1994, nr. 4.

Illustration:
Found on August 2005: http://turkisaretdili.ku.edu.tr/images/cokyasa.gif. Secondary (idadi) School Students from Diyarbakır Sebah & Joaillier, 1890s.

Hand alphabet:
Haydar, Ali, Sagirlar ve Dilsizler, In: Mualimler Mecmuasi, 1925, nr. 29, 1252.

WALES

David Davies, employed as an inspector of education for schools in Wales, discovered to his dismay that there were quite a lot of deaf children in the country who did not receive any education. He mentioned this problem to Hugh Owen, the Minister of State. On 27 December 1846, Owen took up his case and together with Danby Palmer Fry visited the institute for the deaf in London. They wanted to find out if a new school for the deaf in Wales would be feasible. Watson, the director of the institute, referred him to Charles Rhind, the retired teacher of the Ulster Institute for the Deaf in Belfast. Rhind, Owen and Fry jointly wrote the articles of association needed to found an institute for the deaf. Owen and Fry invited Rhind to Wales and he rather liked the idea.

A meeting was held in Aberystwych, the place they believed was the most suitable location for a school. A total of 37 men were willing to donate money towards the school. Three days later they met with the mayor at the town hall. There, it was unanimously decided to set up a school for deaf pupils. The reverend Charles Rhind was appointed as head. In Deaf and Dumb Times, it is read:

> "Born on 5th of October 1813, and privately educated, from an early age Rhind was engaged in teaching Deaf children, being at the age of 16 appointed as a teacher under Dr. Watson at the Old Kent Road School. After 11 years he then moved to Belfast where he was Head of the Deaf School, the Ulster Institution for the Deaf and Dumb, and Blind until 1846, when the Institution moved into new premises. His next move was to Aberystwyth where he founded the first Welsh Deaf School and was its first Principal". Rhind worked there till 1852.

Figure 78: Charles Rhind

On 4 June 1847, after a renovation, the building consisting of a school and a boarding school, opened. It was situated on 17 Pier Street and was rented for £24 a year. The first lessons started on 24 July, for two days a week.

Miss Selina Lewis, former pupil of the institute for the deaf in Edgbaston (England), started her job as a teacher for £25 a year. The method used was a two-handed manual alphabet and manual gestures.

The first pupils were Susannah James and Daniël Jones. During his investigation Tony Boyce, a deaf historian from Doncaster, met some other pupils who in 1847 came over to Aberystwych from the institute for the deaf in York. By the end of the year, the number of pupils grew to eight, among which there were three deaf sisters. The age for admission was from 9 to 13 years.

After a while, a new problem arose: for many pupils from Wales Aberystwych was not so easy to reach as they first

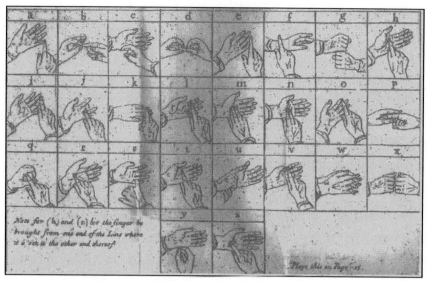

Figure 79: Welsh Hand Alphabet

thought it would be. It was therefore decided in 1850 to move the institute to Swansea, where they also managed to find more donors. This was eventually the main reason for moving to a new location. The Swansea Heritage website mentions that the building of this institute is situated on a hill (Craddock Street).

In 1851, the number of pupils had risen to 50. In 1898, the institution received a royal honor from Queen Victoria, and the school was given a new name: Royal Cambrian Institution for the Deaf.

In 1973, the institute closed for good and two new institutions came in its place: the Ashgrove School at Penarth, administrated by the South Glamorgan Education Authority in South Wales and a second school in Mold (North Wales).[9]

Sources

Content:

Appreciation. In: Deaf and Dumb Times, 1(1), 6.(illus). (England), 1889.

Jackson, Peter, Britain's Deaf Heritage, 62–64. (Edinburgh), 1990.

The Quarterly Review of Deaf-Mute Education, July 1892 – 1894, vol. III, 194–198.

The Silent World, 1959 – 1960, Vol. 14, 148–151.

Boyce, Anthony J. personal correspondence 23 November 2005: his collection on 3 December 2003, in: Archives West Glamorgan on Swansea. It has the records of Cambrian Institution for the Deaf and Dumb, It is under the E/Cam category. (E = Education).

Illustration:

Appreciation. In: Deaf and Dumb Times, 1(1), 6. illus)(England), 1889.

Hand alphabet:

In: Digiti Lingua by Anonymous. (London), 1698.

---

[9] During the ICED2005 conference in Maastricht, Peter Jackson informed me that Wales no longer has any schools or institutes for the deaf. The reason is the practice of mainstreaming, whereby deaf children attend mainstream education in their home towns.

APPENDICES

APPENDIX 1 - QUESTIONNAIRE

The following questionnaire was send to institutes and individuals in 38 European countries:

1. Where and when was the oldest school for the deaf in … founded? (Please state date and year)

2. By whom was the school founded? (Please state name, date and place of birth and date of death)

3. What was the reason for this person to set up the school? By whom were they influenced?

4. What method (manual or oral) was used in the early years?

5. Was there any opposition against this school? If so, by whom?

6. With how many students did the school start?

7. Did the government of your country provide financial and/or moral support?

8. How many schools for the deaf are there currently in your country?

APPENDIX 2 – OVERVIEW OF DEAF SCHOOLS BY COUNTRY

COUNTRIES	FOUNDERS / TEACHERS	YEAR OF FOUNDATION
France	Charles M. de l'Epée (1712 – 1789)	1760
Scotland	Thomas Braidwood (1715 - 1806)	1760
Switzerland	Heinrich Keller (1728 – 1802)	1777
Germany	Samuel Heinicke (1727 – 1790)	1778
Austria	Johann Friedrich Stork (1746 – 1823) Joseph May (1755-1820)	1779
England	Thomas Braidwood (1715 - 1806)	1783
Italy	Tommasso Silvestri (1744 – 1789)	1784
Netherlands	Henri Daniël Guyot (1753 – 1828)	1785
Czech Republic	Karl Berger (1743 – 1806)	1786
Denmark	Georg W. Pfingsten (1746 – 1827) Peter A. Castberg (1779 – 1823)	1787 & 1807
Hungary	András Jólészi Cházár (1745 –1816)	1802
Lithuania	Anzelmas Zigmantas	1805
Spain	J.M. Alea (1781 – 1826) R. F. Prádez (1772 – 1836)	1805
Russia	Czarina Maria Feodorowna (1759 – 1828)	1806
Sweden	Pär Aron Borg (1776 – 1839)	1809
Latvia	Carl August Jakobi	1809 of 1810
Ireland	Charles Edw. H. Orphen (1791–1856)	1816
Poland	Jakub Falkowski (1775 – 1848)	1817
Belgium	Jean-Baptiste Pouplin (1767-1828) Petrus Jozef Triest (1760-1836)	1819 (Wallonia) 1820 – 1822 (Flanders)
Portugal	Pär Aron Borg (1776 – 1839)	1823
Norway	Andreas Ch. Møller (1796 – 1874)	1824

COUNTRIES	FOUNDERS / TEACHERS	YEAR OF FOUNDATION
Northern Ireland	George Gordon	1831
Rumania	Ioan C. Bacila	1831
Slovenia	Valentin Stanic (1774 – 1847)	1840
Finland	Carl Oscar Malm (1826 – 1863)	1846
Wales	Charles Rhind	1847
Estonia	Ernst Sokolovski (1833 – 1899)	1866
Iceland	Páll Séra Pálson (1836 –1890)	1867
Luxemburg	J. Kimmes and Joseph Schuller	1880
Croatia	Adalbert Lampe (deaf) (1842 –1905)	1885
Serbia	Radivoje Popovic	1886
Turkey	Ferdi Garati	1889
Bulgaria	Ferdinand Urbich (1861 – 1945)	1898
Slovakia	Koloman Hercsuth	1906
Greece	American Near-East Foundation	1924
Cyprus	George Markou	1953
Malta	Joe Burlo	1955
Albania	Communist government of Russia	1963

APPENDIX 3 – MANUAL METHOD (SIGN LANGUAGE) VERSUS ORAL METHOD (ORALISM)

The following article is written by Henk Betten to provide an insight in the origin of the discussion on the different communication methods used in deaf education.

Charles Michel de l'Epée and Samuel Heinicke strongly disagreed on the best communication method to transfer knowledge in deaf education: the oral method or the manual method. The oral method is based on the mouth and the use of spoken language and the manual method on the hands and sign language.

Difference

Heinicke was the founder of the so-called German method, which focused on speaking and lip- reading but this method was shrouded in secrecy. It was said that he would only reveal his secret for a large sum of money. This was one of the reasons why after a while many schools for the deaf in Germany no longer used this method. Next to the oral method, Heinicke also used writing and, occasionally gestures but only to support the understanding of the spoken language.

On the contrary, the priest De l'Epée preferred gestures and considered this as a natural language sign language as the native language for his deaf pupils. De l'Epée only taught his pupils how to speak if he considered this necessary. Once a week the priest gave a public lesson, so there was no secrecy in this method.

Dilemma

Stork, a priest and founder of the imperial college for the deaf in Vienna, once told Heinicke that he used sign language as a teaching method. Heinicke subsequently wrote to De l'Epée that he believed that making gestures would have a harmful effect on deaf pupils. He believed that they should only be taught how to speak. In the course of their correspondence, it appeared that they could not reach consensus. De l'Epée eventually decided to put the controversy before several colleges in Europe.

Only the college in Zűrich took the trouble to study the contents of the letters of Heinicke and De l ' Epée. The scholars studied the letters of De l'Epée and Heinicke to find out which method was most suitable to teach deaf children: the manual method or the oral method. The report of the Zűrich Academy was completed in 1783. The conclusion of these scholars was that the manual method was the best method.

Introduction of oralism

In the nineteenth century, the number of schools for the deaf in Europe grew and they used both the oral and the manual method. This changed in 1880. In this year, the Milan conference of teachers in deaf education took place in one of the rooms of the Palais Brescia in Milan. The conference was chaired by Abba Giulio Tarra (1832 – 1889), director of the institute for the deaf in Milan. With the words "Long Live the Spoken Word" this conference officially accepted the introduction of oralism in deaf education in Europe.

The acceptance of the oralism was prompted by the dominant view that deaf children should integrate into society by learning how to speak.

People thought that this would only be possible if the child learned how to speak and read lips. The use of gestures was banned because it was believed that sign language would impede the speech development.

Some institutes changed to the oral method after this Milan Conference, moreover because they received income from donations, which were often subject to certain conditions. This new policy on the oral method took no account whatsoever of the function of sign language in the linguistic development and the welfare of a deaf child.

In the late 20th-century the status of the oral method was lost and sign language was again introduced due to the sign language studies by Stokoe and other scholars. However the oral method is still in use in some countries.

Sources

Bender, Ruth E., The conquest of deafness (Ohio, USA, 1960) 105 - 107

Büchli, M.J.C., De zorg voor de doofstomme (Amsterdam, 1948) 65

Stokoe, William, Sign Language Structure. Library number 7139 Royal Dutch Kentalis. (Silver Spring, Md. , USA), 1960.

Sutermeister, E., Quellenbuch zur Geschichte des Schweizerischen Taubstummenwesens, 815 – 819 (Bern), 1929.

Tervoort, Bernard Th. M., Structurele analyse van visueel taalgebruik binnen een groep dove kinderen. Library number 3347 Royal Dutch Kentalis. (Amsterdam), 1953.

Truffaut, Bernard (France), conversation concerning Milan 1880 during the First European Deaf History Symposium at Rodez, France in 1992.

REFERENCES

Jackson, Peter W. (2004). The Gawdy Manuscripts. Feltham, Middlesex, UK: British Deaf History Society Publications

Rée, Jonathan (2000). I see a voice. A philosophical history of language, deafness and the senses. London: Harper Collins Publishers.

Rietveld-van Wingerden, Marjoke & Tijsseling, Corrie (2010). Ontplooiing door communicatie. Geschiedenis van het onderwijs aan doven en slechthorenden in Nederland. Antwerpen-Apeldoorn: Garant

Stokoe, William (1960). Sign Language Structure. Library number 7139 Royal Dutch Kentalis. Silver Spring, Md., USA

Tervoort, Bernard Th. M. (1953). Structurele analyse van visueel taalgebruik binnen een groep dove kinderen. Library number 3347 Royal Dutch Kentalis. Amsterdam.

Persons register

Alea, José Miguell, 80

Ammann, Johann Conrad, 36, 37, 57, 83

Argillander, Abraham, 81

Arrowsmith, Thomas, 30

August, Friedrich, 40

Bacila, Ioan C., 68

Beda Venerabilis, 30

Berg, 51

Berger, Karl, 26

Beverley, John, 30

Bey, Besim, 85

Bey, Hüseyin Sabri, 85

Björnsdóttir, Camilla Mirja, 45

Bonet, Juan Martin Pablo, 37, 76, 79

Borg, Pär Aron, 66, 81

Bornhaupt, 51

Bourgois, Aloïs, 21

Boyce, Tony, 87

Braidwood, Thomas, 30, 36, 72, 73, 92

Büchli, 31, 38, 42, 43, 49, 50, 59, 80, 83, 84, 95

Bugge, Peter Olivarius, 62

Burlo, Joe, 55

Cardanus, Hieronymus, 49

Carrion, Manuel Ramirez de, 79

Castberg, Peter Atke, 28, 62

Cházár, András Jólészi, 44

Cioranescu, Ion, 68

Clerc, Laurent, 71

Collins, Thomas, 47

Cuyck, Xavier, 21

Czarina Maria Feodorovna, 70

Czech, Franz Herman, 78

Davila, Carol, 68

De l'Epée, Abbé Charles Michel, 15, 18, 36, 57, 83, 94

Deusing, Anthonius, 83

Dircks, Johan Julius, 62

Eglon, Johannes, 32

Ehlert, 51

Ekenstein, Esquire Alberda van, 58

Emmerig, 29, 39, 40, 41, 44, 50, 67, 71, 84

Emperor Joseph II, 26, 27

Empress Catherine the Great of Russia, 37

Empress Thèrese of Austria, 37

Ernaud, Monsieur, 36

Falkowski, Jakub, 64

Fay, Etienne de, 36

Fry, Danby Palmer, 87

Garati, Ferdi, 85

Goodricke, John, 73

Gordon, George, 60

Gordon, Samuel, 60

Green, Francis, 73

Printed in Great Britain
by Amazon